D1176011

OBJECT-ORIENTED SOFTWARE:
Design and Maintenance

SERIES ON SOFTWARE ENGINEERING AND KNOWLEDGE ENGINEERING

Series Editor-in-Chief
S K CHANG (*University of Pittsburgh, USA*)

OBJECT-ORIENTED SOFTWARE: Design and Maintenance

Luiz Fernando Capretz
Miriam A M Capretz

World Scientific
Singapore • New Jersey • London • Hong Kong

Published by

World Scientific Publishing Co. Pte. Ltd.

P O Box 128, Farrer Road, Singapore 912805

USA office: Suite 1B, 1060 Main Street, River Edge, NJ 07661

UK office: 57 Shelton Street, Covent Garden, London WC2H 9HE

Library of Congress Cataloging-in-Publication Data
Capretz, Luiz Fernando, 1950–
    Object-oriented software : design and maintenance / Luiz Fernando
Capretz, Miriam A. M. Capretz.
        p.   cm. -- (Series on software engineering and knowledge engineering ; vol. 6)
    Includes bibliographical references and index.
    ISBN 9810227310
    1. Object-oriented programming (Computer science)   I. Capretz,
Miriam A. M., 1960–   .   II. Title.   III. Series.
QA76.64.C35   1996
005.1'6--dc20   96-21637
                                                                                          CIP

British Library Cataloguing-in-Publication Data
A catalogue record for this book is available from the British Library.

Printed in Singapore.

Foreword

The book by Luiz Fernando Capretz and Miriam A. M. Capretz is a crystallization of the authors' years of effort to present complete software engineering methodologies for object-oriented design and maintenance.

The book covers both theoretical and practical aspects neatly. This is a truly pleasant textbook to read through for conceptual benefit in addition to professional gain. Here, the object-oriented paradigm is beautifully working.

Tosiyasu L. Kunii
President and Professor of Computer Science
University of Aizu, Japan

Preface

The development of software systems is now regarded as among the most complex tasks performed by mankind. The problems that are caused by the scale of this complexity have been recognized for a long time. This complexity affects the costs and time expended on software creation. Moreover, after being built, software systems are often unreliable, difficult to use and, what is worse, they are frequently difficult to maintain and evolve. These difficulties, together with the ever-increasing demand for software, have led to what has become known as the *software crisis*.

An idea which has been receiving a great deal of attention from software engineers is the *object-oriented paradigm*. Currently, this paradigm is thought to be an important aspect of software development, so much so that it has become a major area which is expected to bring significant benefits to software production. The rapid evolution of this paradigm can be attributed to several important reasons, which are discussed in more detail later in this book, but which include: better modelling of real-world applications; better structure for software systems based on abstract data type concepts; and the possibility of reusing software during the creation process.

Despite all of the progress so far in the object-oriented arena, there is a gap in the knowledge concerning software construction. That is, despite the acknowledged importance of software development methodologies and the popularity of object-orientation, there is no generally accepted software methodology that essentially addresses object-oriented development and considers reusability as part of a software life cycle model. From the theoretical and practical viewpoints, the application of object-oriented methodologies remains a topic of major interest.

On the other hand, most books on software engineering has focused mainly on the development phases of the software life cycle; that is, analysis, design and implementation. Until recently, however, software maintenance has been the neglected phase in the software engineering process. The literature on maintenance contains very few entries when compared to the development phases. Little attention has been placed into the subject, and consequently few software maintenance methodologies have been used.

The maintenance of legacy systems (existing software systems) may account for over fifty per cent of all efforts expended by an organization that deals with software. The percentage continues to rise as more software systems are produced. Additionally, as systems age, more effort is likely to be expended on maintenance. Although most legacy systems should be retired or periodically rewritten, this is not always feasible. Since most organizations are gradually becoming more dependent on legacy systems, software maintenance is crucial.

Notwithstanding increasing recognition that maintenance is a major problem during the life cycle of software systems, and acknowledgment of the high costs of maintaining software, there are clearly gaps in the field of software maintenance. So far, there is no generally accepted methodology that systematizes the software maintenance process; neither is there an integrated set of tools which helps tackle the problem of controlling software changes under a methodical scheme.

This book aims at presenting a generic methodology to teach object-oriented design, which considers software reusability as an important aspect of the software life cycle. The main features obtained through the use of an object-oriented design methodology is the creation of a software system following strictly an object-oriented approach, as such a methodology concentrates on identifying and representing classes, inheritance and objects. In doing so, the architecture of an object-oriented software at the design level is built around sets of classes and objects. Moreover, considering reusability as a pragmatic (and desirable!) process within the design phase helps the designer relate software components to each other through relationships which show where a component is defined and used, and in what context. In this way, reusability is encouraged within a software life cycle as part of the object-oriented design methodology.

The book is equally concerned with the description of a general methodology to teach software maintenance. This methodology provides guidelines and procedures for carrying out the maintenance process, while establishing a systematic approach for the support of legacy systems. The methodology takes the software configuration management discipline into account, since this discipline imposes a set of procedures and standards for managing evolving software.

Additionally, there have been a growing interest not only in new methodologies for software development and maintenance, but also the way in which these methodologies can be supported by computerized tools. This technology, known as CASE (Computer-Aided Software Engineering), allows software engineers to document and model a software system from its initial requirements through the design and maintenance stages. Consequently, the ultimate objective for any methodology is that it should be automated by CASE tools. By this means, the rules, principles, guidelines and graphical notations set up by the methodology can be enforced and followed by software engineers, and inconsistencies can be exposed. Ideally, the tools should be integrated into a CASE environment through a common interface together with a single database used to store software information, such as names of classes, attributes, operations and objects, in a uniform representational model.

Aims of the Book

As a book that tackles two important aspects of the software life cycle, i.e. design and maintenance, it gives emphasis to a life cycle model which explicitly recognizes the importance of reusability during the design and maintenance phases. The primary goals of this book are:

- to classify existing object-oriented methodologies according to their suitability for a particular phase of the software life cycle and their application domains. This classification can be used to understand which methodology is best applied to specific phases of the life cycle or certain kinds of systems;

- to present a methodology to teach object-oriented design independent of any other methodology or any programming language. This methodology can be applied to designing software systems which will then conform to object-oriented concepts such as classes, objects and inheritance;

- to offer an alternative software life cycle model within an object-oriented framework, which emphasizes the importance of software reuse during the development and evolution of software;

- to describe a methodology which provides guidelines and procedures for the maintenance process by applying the software configuration management discipline. This methodology improves the balance between source code and higher level abstractions after any change in the software system has been made. As a result, a reliable and easily understandable documentation of an existing software system can be incrementally obtained while it is being maintained;

- to define a software maintenance model, whose phases institute a change control framework to monitor changes. Such a model aims at systematizing the software maintenance process by specifying the chain of events and the order of stages that a change has to go through.

Outline of the Book

The book is organized into eight chapters as follows.

Chapter 1 expands upon the background of the object-oriented paradigm and is divided into six sections. The first section introduces the notions of application domains and solution domains, and shows how object-oriented thinking helps bridge the gap between these two domains. Section 2 discusses the profile of present software in terms of complexity, friendliness, extensibility and reusability. The road towards an object-oriented approach is explained in Section 3, which also presents an overview of the most familiar object-oriented programming languages. Section 4 reviews the main concepts related to object-orientation, and introduces the terminology associated with the object-oriented paradigm to be used in the remainder of this book. The terminology to be presented is independent of any programming language or system. The fifth section introduces the philosophy upon which object-oriented design is based, and examines important issues associated with software construction such as domain analysis, reusability and software life cycle models. A summary of this chapter is given in the sixth section.

Chapter 2 considers a series of classification schemes to assist in the understanding of several existing object-oriented methodologies. The first section compares and contrasts the differences between structured development and object-orientation. The second section introduces the most well-known methodologies, methods and techniques to tackle the analysis and design phases of object-oriented software development. This section discusses the different terminologies employed by them and evaluates their advantages and limitations. Final remarks on this survey are presented in the third section.

Chapter 3 contains a detailed description of a methodology for object-oriented design based on the concepts described in the first chapter. The first section places the methodology into the context of software development. The steps which must be followed in order to design an object-oriented software are discussed in the second section. A means of graphically representing the produced design with a series of different diagrams is explained too. Section 3 gives feedback based on experience with the methodology. The requirements for a CASE environment are examined in the fourth section. The chapter concludes with a review of the methodology steps, outlining issues which must be considered when designing software.

Chapter 4 provides an account of reusability and life cycle issues which arise during object-oriented software production. The first section outlines existing mechanisms to achieve reusability. Besides, it concentrates on the main reasons why software components are not frequently reused and discusses the complications associated with reusability during the design phase. Section 2 puts forward a new software life cycle model that addresses reusability within an object-oriented framework. The section also considers the role of the knowledge about the application domain, and discusses how the knowledge that the designer has about the application domain can affect the creation of software in terms of a top-down, bottom-up or middle-out manner. Some important aspects related to the fully applicability of the presented methodology for object-oriented design within the planned software life cycle model are examined throughout section 3. The chapter finishes with comments on the software process presented in the first two sections.

Chapter 5 expands on the general background of software maintenance and the necessary documentation, as well as introduces the software configuration management discipline to maintain legacy systems. The first section introduces the concepts, problems and categories of software maintenance. Section 2 concentrates on the supporting maintenance technology. In Section 3, the documentation necessary to maintain legacy systems and an approach for incremental documentation are presented. Section 4 looks at the software configuration management discipline, which has been applied mainly to the software development process, as another important factor in helping the maintenance of legacy systems. A summary of this chapter can be found in Section 5.

Chapter 6 describes existing software maintenance models. Section 1 examines the use of models to manage the software life cycle with maintenance. In the second section, a series of software maintenance models, aimed solely at maintaining legacy systems, is presented and compared. The third section introduces the notions and desirable characteristics of software process modelling for software development and maintenance. Section 4 identifies specific points of the software maintenance modelling considered in this book. A summary of this chapter is presented in the fifth section.

Chapter 7 presents a detailed description of a methodology for the maintenance of legacy systems. Section 1 examines the main objectives of such a methodology. In Section 2, a software maintenance model together with its phases is detailed. The role of the software configuration management discipline and the application of each configuration function to the software maintenance methodology are discussed in Section 3. Section 4 details the version control applied to the outcome of the methodology's phases. The chapter concludes with observations on the described methodology.

Finally, Chapter 8 concludes this book by reiterating its main points. Section 1 combines the object-oriented paradigm along with software maintenance. The second section summarizes the methodologies for object-oriented design and maintenance of software systems. The third section provides final remarks on the application of object-orientation. The last section presents an overall conclusion regarding the future of object-oriented software engineering.

Acknowledgments

It is our pleasure to acknowledge some people who have influenced the writing of this book.

We would like to thank Professor Peter A. Lee (University of Newcastle upon Tyne, England) and Professor Malcolm Munro (University of Durham, England) for their comments and constructive criticisms on early drafts of the methodologies put forward in this textbook. We are also grateful to Professor Tosiyasu L. Kunii (University of Aizu, Japan) for allowing us the necessary time to complete this project.

Special thanks are due to our families, in Brazil, for understanding our absence during the moments they most needed us. Their endurance has been really admirable. Our parents, especially, have given us strength and motivation throughout our careers, and for teaching us the meaning of perseverance. Their efforts are greatly appreciated and will never be forgotten.

Luiz Fernando Capretz
Miriam Akemi Manabe Capretz

University of Aizu, Japan
March, 1996

Contents

List of Figures

List of Tables

CHAPTER 1

OBJECT-ORIENTED CONCEPTS

Over the past decades, several software development methodologies have emerged. They address certain phases of the software life cycle ranging from requirements to maintenance. These methodologies have often been created in response to new ideas about how to cope with complexity in software systems. More recently, due to the increasing popularity of object-oriented programming, development of object-oriented methodologies has become a growing field of interest.

There has also been an explosive growth in the number of software described as object-oriented. Some object-oriented ideas have already been applied to various areas such as software engineering, office automation, simulation, virtual reality and multimedia systems. Moreover, programming languages, programming styles and user interfaces have been defined using object-orientation. Consequently, the need for software development methodologies which follows this paradigm has become imperative.

This chapter covers the background of the object-oriented paradigm and is divided as follows. Section 1 presents an introduction to application domains and solution domains. Section 2 discusses the profile of present software systems and shows that object-orientation is suitable to produce such systems. The third section reveals that object-thinking is not new. Actually, it is based on ideas which have been evolving since the early 1970s, and it combines, purifies and evolves existing techniques, such as abstract data types and system simulation. Section 4 reviews the main concepts related to the object-orientation, and introduces the terminology to be used in this book. The fifth section presents the philosophy behind object-oriented design. The chapter ends with a summary of its main topics.

1.1. Application Domains and Solution Domains

In order to attempt to characterize software development methodologies, it is necessary to understand the concept of software in terms of application domains and solution domains. An application domain may be defined as a set of real-world applications. Similarly, a solution domain is a set of possible solutions to those real-world applications. An entity which belongs to an application domain may be mapped into a solution domain through an abstract representation, in such a way that operations on this abstract representation correspond to operations in the real-world application.

As for software, mapping requires the main ideas about a real-world application to be expressed in abstract terms, so that a designer understands the application. The designer can then use those abstractions to develop a model which emulates that real-world application. The mapping may be viewed as a process of building up a model which, when executed by a computer, delivers output that is equivalent to results of the application behaviour. Thus, when the designer thinks about a real-world application in an application domain, there should be a mapping to a solution in a solution domain. The solution might be represented by a software system which simulates the behaviour of that real-world application. The process by which a software system is created may be aided by a software development methodology. Figure 1.1 illustrates such concepts.

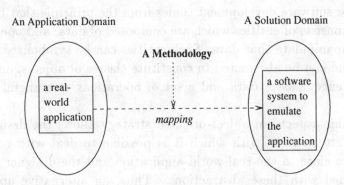

Figure 1.1: Mapping between application and solution domains

Software development methodologies can provide the means by which it is possible to map an abstraction of a real-world application, which belongs to an application domain, into a software representation, which belongs to a solution domain. A software system represents one model of a solution, among possible solutions to that real-world application. Therefore, software development can be seen as a process of creation, manipulation and refinement of representations that model real-world applications. When the designer transforms a representation or creates an initial one, different representations of a software system are being dealt with.

The distance between an application domain and a solution domain is called *semantic gap*. Intuitively, it seems to be evident that the smaller the semantic gap (that is, the closer a software system is to the modelled real-world application) the easier will be the development of that software, and the greater will be the possibility of guaranteeing understandability, reliability and quality in the achieved solution. One of the objectives that should be pursued during the creation of new software development methodologies, programming languages or tools is to narrow the semantic gap as much as possible.

In spite of some advances, for the last twenty years software development has in the main concentrated on procedures and data separately. Unlike other approaches, object-orientation gathers together procedures and data into a unit, named an object. This point of view for software development comes from the principle that the real world consists of entities which are composed of data, and operations which manipulate that data. Such entities can be symbolized by objects and can be abstracted to constitute classes of objects, and each object encompasses data and a set of operations meaningful to the data.

In this aspect, an object-oriented strategy allows the designer to create abstractions with which it is possible to deal with concepts that are close to the real-world application and the designer is only concerned with these abstractions. Thus, an alternative approach based on the identification and manipulation of abstractions represented by classes and objects, and able to narrow the semantic gap, has appeared.

To summarize, during software development, designers should map a real-world application in an application domain onto an abstract solution (represented by a software system) in a solution domain. Using an object-oriented methodology designers can create abstractions in terms of classes and objects. Like other approaches, object-orientation deals with methodologies and languages, both of which systematize the abstraction process to create software, however in this case, classes and objects are the main items used to model real-world applications.

1.2. Profile of Present Software Systems

This section discusses the profile of current software and shows that object-orientation is suitable to develop software systems which satisfy such profile. Some important traits of modern software systems and their requirements include:

- Complexity: the internal architecture of present software systems is complex, often including concurrency and parallelism. Abstraction is a technique which helps to deal with complexity. Abstraction involves a selective examination of certain aspects of an application. It has the goal of isolating those aspects which are important for an understanding of the application, and also suppressing those aspects which are insignificant. An abstraction must have a purpose, because its purpose determines what is and is not relevant for the abstraction. Many different abstractions of the same thing are possible, depending on the purpose for which they are made. Abstracting an application in terms of classes and objects is one of the fundamental notions of object-oriented thinking.

- **Friendliness**: this is an important requirement for current software systems. Iconic interfaces provide a user-friendly interaction between users and software. Icons are graphical representations of objects on the screen and are usually manipulated with the use of a mouse, this has come to be known as *WYSIWYG* (What You See Is What You Get) interaction. In such interfaces, windows, menus and graphical elements are all viewed as objects. The trend to object-oriented graphical interfaces is permeating many areas of software development. This is acknowledged in the most recent generations of software for window management systems. Experience suggests that user interfaces are significantly easier to develop when they are written in an object-oriented fashion. Thus, the object-oriented nature of the WYSIWYG interfaces maps quite naturally into the concepts of the object-oriented paradigm.

- **Extensibility**: this is a property that permits new functionalities to be smoothly added with little modification to existing software systems. With this property, software can be easily extended to meet additional requirements. Extra software development may be carried out entirely by making modifications to what already exists. This incremental development is part of the object-oriented thinking.

- **Reusability**: this property facilitates rapid development by reusing available software components, and also promotes the production of components that could be reused in future projects. Taking components created by others should be considered more desirable than creating new ones. If there exists a good library of reusable components, browsing existing components to identify opportunities for reuse must have precedence over writing new components from scratch. Inheritance is a mechanism that increases software reusability.

There are several ways to tackle the problem of software complexity and to achieve friendliness, extensibility and reusability. Investigations of advanced methodologies, and proposals of new software life cycle models, as well as automated support from tools in a software development environment, have all been under research. These trends may be gathered together and object-orientation seems to be the way to converge them, as can be inferred from the discussions above.

1.3. Towards an Object-Oriented Approach

The notion of object naturally plays a central role in object-oriented software and although this concept is much in evidence nowadays, the idea is not a new one. In fact, it could be said that the object-oriented paradigm was not invented, but it actually evolved by refining existing practices. The confluence of this paradigm with other concepts of computer science suggests that object-orientation has been biased by other fields.

The term object emerged almost independently in various areas of computer science. Some fields that have influenced the object-oriented paradigm are: simulation, operating systems, data abstraction and artificial intelligence. Appearing almost simultaneously in the early 1970s, these approaches cope with software complexity in such a way that objects symbolize abstract components of a software system. For instance, some notions of objects that have emerged from these fields are:

- *Classes* of objects used to simulate a real-world application, in Simula [1]. In this language the running of a computer program is organized as a combined execution of a collection of objects, and objects sharing common behaviour are said to constitute a class.

- Protected resources in operating systems. Hoare [2] proposed the idea of using an enclosed area as a software unit and introduced the concept of a *monitor*, which is concerned with process synchronization and contention for resources among processes.

- Data abstraction in programming languages such as CLU [3]. This refers to a programming style in which instances of *abstract data types* are manipulated by operations that are exclusively encapsulated within a protected region.

- Units of knowledge named *frames*, used for knowledge representation. Minsky [4] proposed the notion of frames to capture the idea that behaviour goes hand-in-hand with the entity whose behaviour is being described. Hence, a frame can also be viewed as an object.

These influences are expressed in Figure 1.2. The common characteristics of these concepts are that an object is a logical or a physical entity which is self-contained. Clearly, other topics could be added to this list, such as advances in programming techniques, including the notion of modularization, as demonstrated in Ada [5].

Simula was the first programming language that had classes and objects as central concepts. Simula was initially developed as a language for programming discrete-event simulations, and objects in the language model entities in the real-world application being simulated. Despite the early innovation of Simula, the term object-oriented became prominent from Smalltalk [6]. This language, first developed in the early 1970s, was greatly influenced by Simula and Lisp. Smalltalk was the software half of an ambitious project known as the Dynabook, which was intended to be a powerful user-friendly personal computer. The Smalltalk language and environment are by-products of that work.

From Smalltalk, some common concepts and ideas have been pointed out and have given support (at least informally) to the object-oriented paradigm which has now established itself. On account of the evolution and dissemination of languages like Smalltalk, this "new"

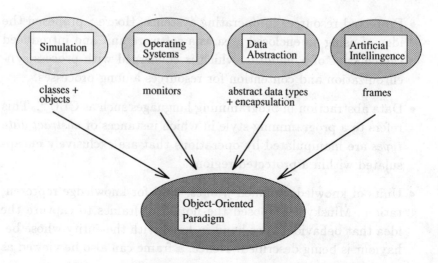

Figure 1.2: Background of the object-oriented paradigm

paradigm has been evolved in several directions, and complementary methodologies, programming languages and tools have appeared. The object-oriented paradigm deals with its own concepts, terminology and notation for software development; these issues are discussed further, later in this chapter. The importance of abstraction and classes to object-orientation will be the focus of the next subsections.

1.3.1. Abstract Data Types

It is easiest to learn new ideas in terms of more familiar ones. Because object-thinking has been strongly influenced by the notion of abstract data types, it is convenient to understand the evolution from this concept to object-orientation. Abstract data types is one of the most important concepts that has emerged from research in programming languages. The term abstract data types refers to an idea in which data structures and related operations to manipulate these data structures are encapsulated within a protected region. A language is said to support abstract data types when it allows the definition of new abstract data types, consisting of declarations that bring together operations and their private data structures.

Abstract data types can be used to introduce extra data types deemed relevant to the application domain. The designer is concerned with the behaviour of these data types and what kind of information can be stored into them and obtained from them. Nevertheless, the designer is not worried about how to implement them. Therefore, designing with abstract data types can be considered as a way of managing complexity as the designer can define and make use of abstract data types without any concern for their internal implementation.

Object-orientation has been influenced by the notion of abstract data types because an object can be viewed as an instance of an abstract data type, encapsulating a data type and supplying a well-defined set of operations to manipulate and access that data type. Actually, in most object-oriented programming languages, a class declaration defines a data type and the operations which can be performed on that data type. Additionally, the concept of abstract data types assumes an important role within an object-oriented framework because it brings others benefits such as modularization and encapsulation, which are also relevant to object-orientation, as examined next.

Modularization

Modularization is inherent to successful development of large software systems because it helps break them into manageable modules. The production of a sizeable software system presents many challenging problems that do not arise when developed via smaller modules. Therefore, the same methods and techniques which work well with small modules do not necessarily apply to large software. Restrictions that merely apply to the size of the modules, however, do not improve the software quality in any real sense, and splitting a big module into a sequence of smaller modules does not necessarily make a software systems any better.

Modularity can be achieved by a collection of abstract data types which the designer thinks belong together, and an interface which specifies the data structures and operations that can be used outside the module. A more helpful notion of modularity refers to the factoring of large software into units that can be modified independently. It means that each module should be understood, and possibly implemented independently of any other modules. Thus, each module must realize a single and simple conceptual functionality of the software system.

Modularization is also associated with the idea of cohesion, which measures the degree of connectivity among modules. The most desirable form of cohesion is functional cohesion, in which modules are closely related and contribute to a particular functionality. A high degree of cohesion is a peculiarity of object-oriented software because classes are naturally cohesive since they encompass operations to achieve a specific purpose.

Encapsulation

Another important concept connected to abstract data types is encapsulation, also known as information hiding. Encapsulation suggests that a data structure must be resident within a module. An interface provides access only to the data structure needed by other modules. Therefore, communication among modules should take place through well-defined interfaces which prevent data structures inside a module from being directly accessed, thus encapsulation minimizes interdependencies among separately written modules.

Parnas [7] has attempted to systematize the modularization process by taking the concept of encapsulation as a criterion for decomposing software systems into modules. Encapsulation as a design principle favours the production of highly independent modules because the state of a module is hidden in its private data structures, visible only within the scope of the module. Once the interface has been carefully defined, modules can be developed independently of each other, stored in a library, combined later to build a unique software system, and reused in future developments.

1.3.2. Evolution of Abstraction in Programming Languages

Abstraction helps cope with complexity. By using an abstraction of an application, someone is able to concentrate only on the important properties of that application. What is relevant depends on the purpose for which the abstraction is being made. As an illustration, someone learning to drive a car may symbolize the car with four properties: an accelerator, a brake, a clutch and a steering wheel. These are abstractions for some visible elements of a car. For a driver, chemical reactions going on inside an engine and the engine itself are irrelevant properties but they would not be for an abstraction made by a mechanic.

In the same way, programs can be seen as abstractions of the computer's central processing unit and memory locations. For instance, in a program to calculate the area of a square, the designer can use self-explanatory names such as `area` and `side`, and perform the operation `side` multiplied by `side`, assigning the result to `area`. With this example in mind the designer is able to split the abstraction of a program into two different aspects: the data and the control aspects. The data aspect models the operands manipulated by programs and the control aspect models the operations performed by programs.

With regard to the first programming languages, assembly languages merely enabled designers to write programs based on machine instructions (operators) which manipulate the contents of memory locations (operands). Therefore, the level of data and control abstractions achieved were very low. A great step forward occurred with the advent of the first high level languages, such as Fortran, Algol and Pascal. The operators turned into statements and operands into variables and data structures.

The conventional view of programs in these languages is that they are composed of a collection of variables which represent some data, and a set of procedures to manipulate these variables. Most traditional programming languages support this data-procedure paradigm. That is, active procedures operate upon passive data that is passed to them. Things happen in a running program by invoking a procedure and passing to it data to be manipulated. Early high level programming languages have reasonable support for expressing actions through statements and procedures, however, they are deficient in representing abstract data types.

Abstract data types are abstractions which exist at a higher level than operands and operators, or variables and procedures separately. The starting point for creating a specification of an abstract data type is to identify the operations on a particular data type. To illustrate, suppose the designer wants to manipulate a *pile* to model a first-in-last-out queue discipline. Two fundamental operations to handle a *pile* are *push* and *pop*. Basically, *push* adds an element to the top of the *pile* and *pop* gets an element from its top. Then the designer could put together into an abstract data type, a *pile* data structure and the operations *push* and *pop* that are relevant to it. More advanced programming languages rely on abstract data types to manage complexity. Some languages such as Simula offer a construct that allows both variables and procedures to be defined in a single unit denominated a class, which enhances the definition of abstract data types. Equivalent ideas can also be found in CLU through the concept of *cluster* and in Ada through the *package* construct.

Object-orientation goes a step further than abstract data types. If two abstract data types are similar but not identical, a programming language which supports only abstract data types provides no means of expressing their commonalities conveniently. However, object-oriented languages allow similarities and differences between abstract data types to be expressed through inheritance, which is the key defining feature of object-thinking. Therefore, it would be better to understand the evolution of object-oriented languages in terms of abstract data types and inheritance; in this case the immediate ancestor of object-oriented languages is Simula, an Algol-based language, which first introduced the notion of class. Besides, as object-oriented concepts have also arisen from the artificial intelligence community, it is not surprising that Lisp has influenced a number of object-oriented languages as well. Some of them are Flavors [8], Loops [9] and CLOS [10], which have borrowed ideas from both Lisp and Smalltalk.

The prominence of such a paradigm has influenced the definition of other languages as well. There has been serious work to add object-oriented constructs to the popular C, Pascal and Modula-2 languages, resulting in the hybrid languages Objective-C [11], C++ [12], Object-Pascal [13] and Modula-3 [14]. The addition of object-orientation into traditional languages has sophisticated them, in that, programmers have the flexibility to use or not the object-oriented extensions and their benefits. Although these hybrid languages have become more complex, such extensions have given a helping hand to programmers who have considerable experience with these traditional languages, to explore incrementally the different ideas provided by object-oriented thinking. Nevertheless, when using a hybrid language, programmers must exercise more discipline than those using a pure object-oriented language because it is quite easy to deviate from sound object-oriented principles. For example, C++ permits the use of global variables, which violates the fundamental principle of encapsulation.

As far as concurrency is concerned, objects can also be defined as concurrent agents interacting by message passing, emphasizing the role of entities such as actors and servers in the architecture of the real-world application. The main idea behind object-oriented languages that support concurrency is to give designers powerful constructs that allow objects to run concurrently. Concurrency adds the idea of simultaneously executing objects, exploiting parallelism on a large scale. Languages with this purpose include Actor [15], POOL-T [16] and Mushroom [17].

Other languages, such as Beta [18], Trellis/Owl [19] and Eiffel [20], have appeared (influenced basically by Simula, CLU and Smalltalk) and are believed to give good support for the object-oriented paradigm. Although Smalltalk, and Eiffel seem to be the most coherent object-oriented languages and come with an integrated programming environment, it is more likely that C++ will continue to be the object-oriented language most used in the near future because of its portability and efficiency, along with the influence of the UNIX operating system, and the popularity of C from which C++ has been derived. However, C++ still requires a more robust programming environment to manage library of classes. An analysis of the evolution of these languages over the past decades results in the dependency graph shown in Figure 1.3.

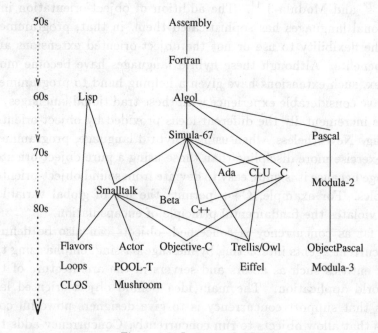

Figure 1.3: Language evolution

1.3.3. Comparison of Selected Object-Oriented Languages

Because object-oriented design evolved naturally from object-oriented programming, it is helpful to study the characteristics of a few languages to realize how the influence on design emerged. As discussed above, object-thinking has been incubated in several languages, and over the last decade a number of object-oriented languages have come out. In this subsection a few so-called object-oriented languages are briefly reviewed and compared, and their main features outlined.

Object-oriented programming has been explained in such a way that any language in which a particular unit has a state, and applicable operations associated with it, is said to be an object-oriented language. Nowadays, there is an attempt to delineate object-oriented programming by examining the presence or lack of specific programming aspects, such as messages passing and inheritance. But, what properties must a programming language have, to be considered object-oriented?

A programming language is designated `object-based` if it is based only on objects. Nevertheless, a language is denominated `object-oriented` if it provides linguistic support for objects and additionally requires that objects are instances of classes. Moreover, inheritance must be supported. Hence:

```
object-oriented = classes + objects + inheritance
```

According to this definition, a set of object-based languages would include Ada and CLU because objects in Ada are supported by packages, and in CLU by clusters. Theoretically, the set of object-oriented languages is narrower than the set of object-based languages, and would exclude languages such as Ada and CLU but would include languages such as Smalltalk and C++ because the latter two support inheritance.

Another different characterization of object-oriented languages to be presented here is rather informal, but seems appropriate for the object-orientation as a whole. It is claimed that an object-oriented language should support abstract data types, inheritance, dynamic binding and it is also relevant whether all manipulated items are objects. Dynamic binding allows great flexibility to handle objects at run-time and is one of the major reasons for the flexibility of object-oriented languages. In addition, library support, which is not part of the language definition but beneficial for object-oriented software development has been considered.

Clearly, some languages are better fitted than others for object-thinking. For example, Smalltalk renders transparent ways to work within an object-oriented framework only, but Ada may be used in an object-oriented manner with a few tricks. The main point is how far a particular language naturally embodies and enforces the properties of classes, objects and inheritance.

Simula

Many of the ideas behind object-oriented languages have roots going back to Simula [21], which introduced the notion of class as a mechanism for encapsulating variables and procedures. In Simula, a class X can be a specialization of another class Y. That is, X inherits all local variables and procedures of Y. Additionally, X can add variables and procedures of its own. Simula is a general purpose language that supports abstract data types, single inheritance and dynamic binding. It is a strongly-typed language but does not afford library facilities nor multiple inheritance.

CLU

CLU [3] was motivated by a desire to support generic mechanisms to specify abstract data types and make their representation completely encapsulated, in such a way that user-defined abstract data types are treated as similarly as possible to built-in types. An abstract data type in CLU is implemented by a language construct labeled *cluster* which identifies a set of data structures and a set of operations to manipulate these data structures. In this aspect, CLU made a serious effort towards object-orientation.

Ada

Ada [5] is a general purpose language defined primarily to enforce software engineering principles of abstraction, encapsulation and modularity. Ada is not really an object-oriented language for the purists. It has a construct, namely *package*, which can be used to denote a class and gives an object-oriented flavour. However, in Ada there are serious limitations to create additional abstract data types by specializing existing ones. This weakness results in the impracticability of using inheritance. Ada is a strongly-typed language that performs all binding at compile-time, but there is a reasonable support for library facilities.

Smalltalk

Following the introduction of Simula and CLU, a number of languages that support abstract data types have been introduced. Despite earlier languages containing object-oriented ideas, the term object-oriented itself is generally associated with Smalltalk [22]. More than a language, Smalltalk is a complete programming environment composed of an object-oriented language kernel, a persistent programming system and a user-friendly interface. Although Lisp influenced Smalltalk and the notion of class came from Simula, many concepts were born with it, such as *methods* to manipulate objects, and message passing between objects. The radical difference between Smalltalk and previous languages is that in Smalltalk everything is considered as objects, from the primitive language types like integers and characters to user-defined types such as graphics and windows.

In Smalltalk, there is one basic unit (i.e. an object) that embodies variable declarations and method definitions. Every object is an instance of some class. Smalltalk also supports inheritance, permitting a hierarchy of classes to be built. All variables and methods of an object are specified in the class of that object, or in its superclasses. The top level superclass is termed *Object*. All classes are refinements of the *Object* superclass in that they add different methods or allow new variables in their instances. Classes themselves are objects and as a consequence instances of other special classes named *meta-classes*.

Smalltalk objects interact by exchanging messages. In addition to message passing, different objects of a class can share variables, denominated *class variables*. Class variables are defined in a meta-class and are accessible to any method in that class. Smalltalk supports automatic garbage collection, which means that the lifetime of all objects is determined not only by the programmers but also by the environment. It provides excellent information hiding, dynamic binding and an extensive library that encourages prototyping and reuse of existing classes.

Objective-C

Two separate efforts bring the benefits of object-orientation available to programmers trained in the C programming language. Objective-C [11] and C++ [12] are both hybrid languages, planned as extensions of the C language and as such have C characteristics such as efficiency and portability. Although the aims of both languages are similar, they differ significantly in that Objective-C adds Smalltalk constructs to C, whereas C++ shows a clear Simula influence. In fact, Objective-C is a superset of C, that is, it kept C features and included object-oriented basic concepts. To be more precise, Objective-C puts the notions of class, inheritance and dynamic binding into C. With Objective-C the term *Software-IC* has been introduced as a reusable software component.

C++

As far as C++ [12] is concerned, it is a general purpose language and also a superset of the C programming language. Objects in C++ are instances of some class. Variables and functions are referred to as the *members* of a class. A member can be *public*, *private* or *protected*. A public member can be accessed by both members and non-members of a class. A private member is accessible only to other members of the class, and protected members are accessible to other members of the class and its subclasses. A *constructor* is a special operation used to create and initialize objects. On the other hand, another special operation named *destructor* can be invoked to destroy an object. Inheritance is used to implement *derived* classes, which have the refined commonalities of some other *base* classes.

Assuming that the learning curve from C to C++ is not steep but significant, the real hurdle of using C++ has to do more with object-oriented programming style [23] than with language syntax. For someone who knows C, the real advantage of C++ is that new programming features can be learned incrementally (or corrupted gradually!). This is advantageous for some, but unfortunate for others who claim that there is a danger of cheating and reverting to procedural programming using an object-oriented language.

CLOS

In the 1980s a number of languages merged concepts of Lisp with Smalltalk. Flavors [8] and Loops [9] were derived from Lisp with object-thinking built on top, and followed the same ideas praised by Smalltalk; both renders multiple inheritance, but not library facilities. Through the experience derived from Flavors and Loops, another object-oriented language called CLOS [10] has been derived. CLOS is also a Smalltalk-like language based on the notions of class, metaclass, method and multiple inheritance. A common criticism that can be made on these languages is that, due to the strong Lisp influence, all of them have qualities useful to basically deal with artificial intelligence applications.

ObjectPascal

ObjectPascal [13] is an object-oriented clone of Pascal, which defines a class as an extension of the *record* structure. In this language a module is termed *unit*. A unit is divided into an interface part and an implementation part, both can be compiled separately. The greatest strength of ObjectPascal is its simplicity, which attempts to streamline the language learning process.

Beta

Beta [18] is a language in the Simula tradition. A program in Beta is regarded as a simulation of an application modelled by interacting objects. Beta replaces the class and type notions by another very general and abstract concept named *pattern*, which can also be organized into a classification hierarchy by means of *sub-patterns*. However, Beta does not support multiple inheritance. An object in Beta is described by a set of attributes that portrays the properties of the object, and a sequence of actions. Finally, patterns may be checked at compile time, even though the binding is done at run-time.

Eiffel

Eiffel [20] is a pure and clean object-oriented language that shares the best properties of other languages described above by offering single and multiple inheritance, generic classes and dynamic binding. Besides, the language combines object-orientation with expressions for formal program verification such as assertions and invariants. The language also caters statements for exception handling, that is, treatment of abnormal conditions (exceptions) in order to guarantee software fault tolerance. In fact, Eiffel is an environment geared towards the production of sizable software systems strongly encouraging reuse of components from its library.

Trellis/Owl

Trellis/Owl [19] consists of a programming environment called Trellis, glued to an object-oriented language named Owl. Trellis is composed of several user-friendly tools to support editing, compiling and debugging. Owl enforces abstraction, supports multiple inheritance and comes with an extensive library of reusable components. Like Smalltalk and Eiffel, Trellis/Owl affords an excellent support for object-orientation.

Table 1.1 shows a comparison among the selected object-oriented languages. In this table, 'y' points that the feature is present in the language or environment, whereas 'n' indicates that it is absent.

Some of these currently used programming languages support object-orientation better than others, however, the perspective on the paradigm is as important as the language statements. In other words, it is possible to think in object-oriented terms without a language

Table 1.1: Comparison among object-oriented languages

Features vs Languages	Abstract Data Types	Single Inheritance	Multiple Inheritance	Dynamic Binding	All are Objects	Library Support
Simula	y	y	n	y	n	n
CLU	y	n	n	y	n	n
Ada	y	n	n	n	n	y
Smalltalk	y	y	n	y	y	y
Objective-C	y	y	n	y	n	y
C++	y	y	y	y	n	y
CLOS	y	y	y	y	y	n
ObjectPascal	y	y	n	y	n	n
Beta	y	y	n	y	n	n
Eiffel	y	y	y	y	y	y
Trellis/Owl	y	y	y	y	y	y

that enforces the paradigm, however, the main point is not to force the language to deal with concepts that are not naturally supported. Although it is possible to adhere to object-orientation even using procedural languages [24] such as C and Pascal, they are not as suitable for object-oriented programming as Smalltalk, Eiffel, or C++ are.

A language is said to support a programming paradigm if it provides facilities that make it easy, safe and efficient to use the paradigm. On the other hand, a language does not support a paradigm if it takes exceptional efforts, skills or artifices to follow that paradigm. It means that support for a programming paradigm must come not only in the obvious form of language properties which allow straight use of the paradigm, but also in the more subtle form of compile-time and run-time checks against unintentional deviation from the paradigm.

It can also be concluded that, despite the possibility of following object-orientation using those languages (shown in Table 1.1) with less or more difficulty, direct language support is beneficial in order to facilitate and encourage the use of an object-oriented way, such as in Smalltalk or Eiffel. Not only do these languages support object-thinking, but they also enforce it because the main concepts dealt with are classes and objects. The danger in trying to force object-thinking into a language (e.g. as in Ada) which does not compel to object-oriented ideas is that inconsistent constructions may be produced, impairing software development and jeopardizing the quality of the resulting software.

1.4. Characterization of an Object-Oriented Model

Although the object-oriented paradigm has its roots in the 1970s, there have been lots of discussions about what precisely the term object-oriented means. It means different things to different people because it has become very fashionable labeling any modern software system as object-oriented.

To some authors, the concept of object is merely another name for abstract data types; each object, like an abstract data type, has its own private variables and local procedures, resulting in modularity and encapsulation. To others, classes and objects are a concrete form of type theory. In this view, each object is considered as an instance of a class which itself can be related through subtype and supertype relationships to several classes. To others still, the object-thinking is a way of organizing and sharing source code; procedures and the data they manipulate are arranged into a tree structure. Objects at any level of this tree inherit behaviour of higher level objects; inheritance is the main structuring mechanism that makes it possible for similar objects to share source code.

Despite many authors being concerned with finding a precise definition for the object-oriented paradigm, it is difficult to come up with a single, generally accepted one. This paradigm is not something that can be easily cordoned off. In fact, these attempts have been used as a way to lead the discussions, rather than formally define the paradigm. Therefore, it would be fairer to characterize an object-oriented approach for software development, as will be seen later in this section.

Rentsch [25] and Thomas [26] explain object-oriented programming in terms of inheritance, encapsulation, methods and messages. Indeed, they have been influenced by Smalltalk. Objects are uniform in that all items are objects and no object properties are visible to an outside observer. All objects communicate using the same mechanism of message passing, and processing activity takes place inside objects. Inheritance permits classification, subclassification and superclassification of objects, which allows their properties to be shared.

Nygaard [27] considers object-oriented programming taking as a basis the notion of objects as in Simula. In that language the execution of a computer program is seen as the joint execution of a collection of objects. The collection as a whole simulates a real-world application, and objects sharing common properties are said to constitute a class. Nygaard regards object-oriented programming as a model that simulates the behaviour of either a real or imaginary part of the real world. The model consists of objects determined by attributes and actions, and the objects simulate phenomena. Any transformation of a phenomenon is reflected by actions on the attributes. The state of an object is expressed by its attributes and the state of the whole model is the state of the objects in that model.

Lastly, Wegner [28] defines an object-oriented approach in terms of objects, classes, inheritance and abstract data types. Objects are autonomous entities which respond to messages or operations and have a state; classes determine objects by their common operations; inheritance serves to classify classes by their shared behaviour; and abstract data types hide the representation of data and the implementation of operations. The characterization of an object-oriented style by Wegner is closest to the one to be presented in this book.

As it has been shown, there are various interpretations of the object-oriented paradigm. Nevertheless, one thing that all definitions have in common, not surprisingly, is the recognition that object is the primitive concept for object-orientation. Therefore, it is better to characterize what the term object means before starting using it. Curiously though, it has been notoriously difficult to capture precisely what is meant by an object. In fact, there are two important aspects with which the object-orientation deals: the first is an object-oriented model composed of objects, classes and inheritance mechanism (discussed in the next subsections), and the second is the philosophy of object-oriented design (considered in the next section).

The object-oriented model comprises a collection of principles which forms the foundation of the object-oriented paradigm. The next subsections cover the concepts, features and mechanisms common to this paradigm and set the terminology to be used in the remainder of this book.

1.4.1. Objects

An *object* is an encapsulation of some state together with a defined set of operations on that state. An object embodies an abstraction of an entity in the real world. Hence, it exists in time, it may have a changeable state and can be created and destroyed. An object has an identity (which is a distinguishing characteristic of an object) that denotes a separate existence from other objects. The object's behaviour characterizes how an object acts and reacts in terms of changes in its state. In fact, each object can be viewed as a computer endowed with a memory and a central processing unit, and able to provide a service.

1.4.2. Classes

A *class* is a template description which specifies properties and behaviour for a set of similar objects. Every object is an instance of only one class. A class may have no instances (usually labeled *abstract class*). Every class has a name and a body that defines the set of attributes and operations possessed by its instances (objects). Note that the term *object* is sometimes used to refer to both class and instance (especially in languages where a class is itself an *object*). However, it is important to distinguish between an object and its class; here the term class is used to identify a group of objects and the term object to mean an instance of a class.

Attributes and *operations* are usually part of the definition of a class. Attributes are named properties of an object and hold abstract states of each object. Operations characterize the behaviour of an object, which is expressible in terms of the operations meaningful to that object. The operations are the only means for accessing, manipulating and modifying the attributes of an object. An object communicates with another through a *request*, which identifies the operation to be performed on the second object. The object responds to a request by possibly changing its attributes or by returning a result. An *interface* comprises of the set of operations that can be requested by other objects; the external view of an object is nothing more than its interface.

Figure 1.4 represents a real-world entity denominated dictionary mapped in terms of object-oriented concepts. Attention must be paid to the difference between the *DICTIONARY* class and one of its possibly instantiated objects labeled *EnglishDictionary*. A class serves as a template for its instances.

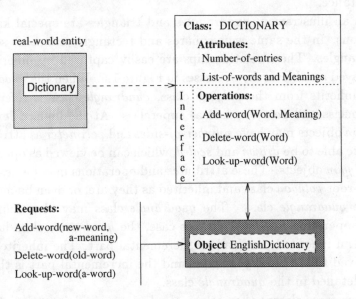

Figure 1.4: Concepts related to the object-oriented paradigm

By using the concepts of classes and objects as stated above important characteristics, such as abstraction, encapsulation and modularity are achieved. These features are recognized as being peculiarities of good quality software, therefore object-orientation, in theory, encourages the development of high quality software.

1.4.3. Inheritance

The *inheritance* mechanism can be used to represent a relationship between classes. It is a mechanism for sharing commonalities (in terms of attributes and operations) between classes. Every inheritance relationship has parents designated the *superclasses* and children denominated the *subclasses*, and attributes and operations inherited. When a subclass inherits commonalities from one superclass only, this is called *single inheritance*. When a subclass inherits commonalities from two or more superclasses, this is termed *multiple inheritance*. Hence, single inheritance is a particular case of multiple inheritance.

As an illustration, quadrangles and triangles are special kinds of polygons. In the same way, squares and rectangles are some sorts of quadrangles. These relationships are easily captured by inheritance, portrayed as a hierarchy of classes in Figure 1.5. When the *quadrangle* class inherits from the *polygon* class, *quadrangle* class is referred to as subclass and *polygon* class as superclass. At the highest level, all *polygon* objects may have *number-of-sides* and *perimeter* as attributes, and are able to be *drawn* and *scaled*, which can be viewed as operations on *polygon* objects. These attributes and operations may be described in the root *polygon* class and inherited as they are, or even be modified in the *quadrangle* class. The *quadrangle* class may also define the *rotate* operation for itself. In this case, the *quadrangle* class has two parts, an inherited part and an incremental part. The inherited part is derived from the *polygon* class and the incremental part is the new part detailed in the *quadrangle* class.

Therefore, classes themselves can be organized into class hierarchies. Such class hierarchies allow similar classes to be related together in such a way that commonalities of one class can be inherited (reused) rather than duplicated by classes lower in the hierarchy, thus simplifying the design and implementation of these lower level classes.

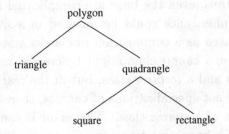

Figure 1.5: Hierarchy representing inheritance

Problems with Inheritance

Inheritance is a powerful mechanism but gives rise to complex issues including overriding of inherited commonalities and lack of semantic relationship between classes. The occurrence of multiple inheritance is much more complicated than the single one because the former creates ambiguity between names of attributes and operations; this increases the likelihood of errors. Moreover, when multiple inheritance is used, there is more risk of introducing meaningless and redundant attributes into the subclasses. This can lead to the creation of a conceptually confusing class hierarchy.

A deep evaluation of inheritance also reveals that it can cause violation of encapsulation because by using inheritance a subclass may access or refer to an attribute of its superclass and an operation in a subclass can call another operation in its superclass. The trouble is that instead of gathering attributes and operations together, the class hierarchy scatters them among superclasses and subclasses. Therefore, rather than isolating the effect of a change in a class hierarchy, inheritance increases dependencies between its superclasses and subclasses. Changes undertaken on superclasses are potentially difficult to manage because modifications inside a superclass within a class hierarchy affect all subclasses which have that superclass as root. Thus the use of inheritance does not isolate the effects of changes in attributes and operations. On the contrary, it replicates the effects of a change. Those more skeptical could say that "inheritance is so good that hides all details, even the bugs are complicated to find".

In addition, inheritance could be misused in a situation where a superclass is created as a composition of classes, not as a specialization. To illustrate, a *course* class might be created as an aggregation of a *student* class and a *lecturer* class, but in the real world, students and lecturers are not specializations of courses, therefore they should not be subclasses of a *course* class. This error is caused by the misunderstanding of a `has-a` relationship as a `is-a` relationship [29]. The `has-a` relationship takes place when an entity is part of another, for example, an airplane has wings. On the other hand, the `is-a` relationship happens if an entity is a specialization of another, for instance, a worker is a person.

The use of inheritance is sometimes acceptable but not recommendable when it does not reflect concepts in the real world. As an illustration, an ellipse determined by two focii and one radius is not a specialization of a circle defined by one focus and one radius. Actually, a circle is a specialization of an ellipse because a circle has two coincident focii. Objects of a subclass should always be objects of the superclass. The subclass is more specific than the superclass, not the opposite. This problem can easily occur, as it comes about in the class hierarchy drafted in Figure 1.5. The *square* class could have been placed as a subclass of the *rectangle* class. Squares are more specific than rectangles, as a square is just a special rectangle with four equal sides. Every square is a rectangle but not the other way round. Can the reader modify Figure 1.5 and include a *diamond* class?

In the context of this book, inheritance is defined as a mechanism for a hierarchical classification of attributes and operations at design level, and resource sharing at implementation level. Since commonalities can be shared by means of inheritance, a library of reusable components is typical during object-oriented software development as will be seen in Chapter 4.

1.5. Philosophy of Object-Oriented Design

Object-orientation is an idea to software development in which the design of a software system is based on the creation of collections of classes that map entities of a real-world application into a software solution. The real-world entities are subsequently simulated in a computer by corresponding software objects that mirror the behaviour of their real-world counterparts. The design process, in itself, should be independent of any particular programming language, and so must be a general design methodology.

The vast majority of designers are used to thinking in terms of functional decomposition, which emphasizes functions and processes, rather than in terms of classes and objects, which characterize object-oriented design. As a result, when these designers first try object-orientation, they map the functions they would have created directly onto objects. They also have other difficulties such as mapping system behaviour with wrong objects, or creating class hierarchies that poorly correspond to the real-world application. The problem is that such designers are not skilled in how to apply object-orientation.

Other designers suggest that a good way to find classes for an object-oriented software is to start from a natural language description of the software requirements and to underline nouns that will represent objects. To illustrate, a sentence from a requirements description of the form "the radar must track the position and speed of an incoming airplane" would lead a designer to detect the need for two objects, *radar* and *airplane*.

This is just a simple minded technique, and it can merely give rough first results. For instance, it is not clear if two other nouns in the sentence, *position* and *speed*, should also be identified as separate objects or attributes of an *airplane* object. A better tactic is to make use of the idea behind abstract data types, that is, an abstraction should only be made into a class if it describes a group of objects marked by purposeful operations and meaningful attributes. So, should the position of an airplane yield a class or not? If there are no specific operations on *position*, then it should be an attribute of an *airplane* class. Alternatively, if *position* is a significant entity with associated operations (e.g. distance to another point or conversion to another coordinate system) then it is worthwhile defining a *position* class.

Despite the importance of creating a model of the software system during design, current object-oriented design methodologies have not highlighted how to construct a design model based only on classes, objects and inheritance. Designers using these methodologies are often faced with the following daunting tasks:

- What is the best strategy to decompose a software system?

- Where do classes and objects come from?

- Which operations perform a required functionality?

These questions have been posed to designers of object-oriented software for a long time. Unfortunately, the consensus among designers has been that it is difficult to find the right classes and objects. Nevertheless, a design methodology can help answer these questions because it provides rules and guidelines to build a design model composed of classes and objects, systematizing the whole design process.

Building a design model is an activity of fundamental importance because the efficiency of the design process and the quality of the final software greatly depend on the clarity, completeness and consistency of the design model. The representation of a design model may consist of narrative and graphical descriptions. Certain diagrams are believed to be useful to describe a design model. For instance, class diagrams show hierarchies among classes, and object diagrams can depict communications between objects.

The best way to characterize the philosophy behind object-oriented design is to centralize the design process on the notions of classes and objects. That is, similar objects in an application are abstracted as classes in a software solution; properties of the objects are designated as attributes and operations, and communications between objects are denoted as requests. Relationships between classes are reflected in class hierarchies; classes with common properties are generalized into a superclass; classes are specialized into subclasses as well. This process can be repeated and, as a result, several class hierarchies may emerge.

The philosophy of object-oriented design is inspired by three different ways in which designers can structure their knowledge about an application:

1. Classification and instantiation.

2. Generalization and specialization.

3. Decomposition and composition.

Classification and instantiation help organize objects into classes because a class is a set of objects sharing common properties; classification of objects leads to classes, whereas instantiation of classes leads to objects. Typically, classification starts by identifying properties shared by more than one object in a given design. Identification of common properties depends on the intended use of the objects. The objects which share the same properties are grouped together into classes and regrouping may occur several times until a set of classes becomes stable.

Generalization and specialization bring out the notions of superclass and subclass. These closely related concepts provide much of the power of the object-oriented paradigm. Generalization supports the exploitation of commonalities between classes. When two or more classes introduce overlapping sets of attributes and operations, the commonalities can be factored out of both classes and used to create a new superclass with those previously overlapping commonalities. Specialization guides designers in the reuse of existing abstractions by defining supplementary subclasses that are more specific than the existing classes. The sequence of creating class hierarchies may vary. A superclass may be created first and then the subclasses, or vice versa.

Decomposition and composition are two important mechanisms used during the design process. Decomposition divides a large component into smaller and simpler components that may then be refined independently. With object-orientation, decomposition is based on classes and objects. In contrast, small components can be aggregated and evolve incrementally into larger components through composition.

During object-oriented design a hierarchy of classes may be built from general to specific, from specific to general or through a mixture of both fashions. The first path starts from a general class and through specialization reaches subclasses, and eventually objects. The second path starts with objects or subclasses, from which properties are generalized into superclasses. Classification, instantiation, generalization and specialization may be used to structure and rearrange existing classes into new ones or into class hierarchies. In fact, a combination of these styles is more likely to be used, depending on what designers know best; whether classes as a whole or some objects. These issues are further examined in Chapter 4.

1.5.1. Domain Analysis

Domain analysis attempts to identify and classify entities and to search for interrelationships perceived important within an application domain. Such identification and classification of entities may arise from the vocabulary used in that application domain, usually in the form of keywords and semantic relationships between those entities. To illustrate, a process control system for a chemical plant is concerned with the vessels, pipes and valves of the plant, as well as the flow of liquid and gases, the temperature and pressure at various points in the plant. A payroll system is concerned with employees, the pay they earn, the tax they must pay, and the holidays they are entitled to. The identification and classification of entities help establish important relationships between them, which can be connected and organized according to their semantic meaning in that application domain.

Domain analysis and object-orientation are closely related. The domain analysis process can yield an initial set of classes reflecting the main conceptual entities within an application domain. Therefore, essential properties of the application domain are captured and initial candidates for classes emerge. Consider for example the application domain of airline reservation systems. Typical entities of these systems are: seats, flights, crews and passengers; and interrelationships can be: reserve a seat to a passenger, assign a crew to a flight, schedule a flight, and so on. These real-world entities and interrelationships are likely to become classes or operations in the software system.

Relatively little work has been done in the area of object-oriented domain analysis. Perhaps the most significant work has been carried out within the Ithaca [30] environment, where a range of object-oriented tools for early software development has been created. Ithaca aims at building an environment to support the development of object-oriented software in a variety of application domains. The environment includes:

- An object-oriented language with database support.

- A software information database to store and manage knowledge concerning reusable software and its intended use.

- A selection tool for browsing and querying the software information database.

- A variety of application development tools built around the software information database.

The main idea behind Ithaca is to make provision for an environment that supports software engineers in developing and maintaining software systems in a number of different selected application domains. Instead of focusing on the individual application, the goal is to produce workbenches containing software components and generic application frameworks which characterize the software systems of a particular application domain.

The components resulted from domain analysis are better suited for reuse because they capture the essential functionality required in the application domain. Thus, designers find these components easier to include in new software systems in that application domain. The key issue is a careful domain analysis in order to identify the basic components within the application domain and, if possible, reuse them from a library of reusable components. Chapter 4 presents a method for domain analysis that produces a collection of reusable components specific to an application domain.

1.5.2. Reuse of Software

Reusability is the practice of incorporating existing components into software systems for which they were not originally intended. Reusability is an important area of software engineering and holds the promise of improving software quality and reducing development costs and schedules; as a result, reusability can bring about great improvements in productivity. It is likely to be more cost effective spending some time searching for a reusable component rather than defining, implementing and testing a new component created from scratch.

In the past, the idea of reusability was linked with copying source code or invoking subroutines from a library. Therefore, reuse of software has been usually performed at the implementation phase. However, reuse of source code during the implementation phase is a very limited kind of reusability. Besides, it is too late to consider reusability just at the implementation phase. Greater benefits are obtained when reusability occurs at more conceptual levels. From the beginning of the software life cycle, designers should be aware of potentially reusable components as achieving reusability at domain analysis and design stages will certainly influence the implementation phase. At a higher level than implementation, reusability involves a classification of components, which gives the information on components' functionalities; as well as accessibility, which allows a component to be searched for, retrieved and hence reused.

There are many reasons for disappointments regarding design with reuse. Most of the problems are centered around the difficulties of classifying software components and searching for potentially reusable components. Furthermore, reusability is inhibited by a high initial amount of time required to explore libraries of reusable components (reusable libraries), which may also involve accessing components and adapting them if necessary. Components might have a lot of characteristics which need to be understood, and this is, of course, time consuming. Another relevant factor that hinders reusability is that many software development environments do not have an automated support for reusable libraries, and those which have, suffer from a steep learning curve because the components were not explicitly designed for reuse.

Additionally, there are complications involving the design of components for reuse. For example, there is a conflict between the need to develop components on schedule for use in a particular software system or to take additional time to make them generic for possible reuse in future developments. Therefore, reusable components require further effort to make them generic and robust.

Reusability throughout the entire software life cycle is an idea that has appealed to software engineers for a long time [31]. Unfortunately, reuse of software has proven to be a complex task affected by many factors. The infamous not-invented-here syndrome is particularly apparent when dealing with reuse. Architectural mismatch [32] between what is needed and what is available. Frakes and Fox [33] ask intriguing questions about software reuse, and answer them using empirical data as a basis. Besides, Tracz [34] exposes some myths about reusability. Despite all these discussions, the literature presents successful experience on design for reuse [35] and software development with reuse [36].

Reusability during Object-Oriented Design

The ability to support reuse of software is an important aspect of the object-oriented paradigm. This paradigm encourages reusability rather than reinvention because it naturally embodies some advantages such as:

- Classes and objects are good abstractions of concepts present in real-world applications.

- Classes and objects support modularity and encapsulation.

- Reusable classes can be easily stored in and retrieved from libraries.

- Classes can be specialized by subclassifying, and both attributes and operations can be reused in subclasses.

- Classes can be organized into frameworks to serve as templates to a particular application domain.

When an existing class is not exactly what is required for a developing software system, designers should try to customize that class in a manner to fit its new purposes. There are three ways of performing such customization:

1. Modify the original class definition.

2. Make a copy of the original class and modify the copy.

3. Modify the original class by augmentation.

The problem with the first solution is that the original class becomes more complicated as it is tailored for use in several applications. The modification usually consists of a `case` statement that executes a different path depending on which application is currently using such a class. This creates classes difficult to understand and to extend, and it is against object-orientation. As far as the second solution is concerned, modifying a copy of a class brings an updating problem, because replicated changes are not usually made automatically to all copies. The third alternative is achieved with inheritance where a new subclass is defined by detailing the difference between this new subclass and its pre-existing superclass, and appending the fresh subclass to the old superclass by making the former a specialization of the latter.

A good example of reusability can be found within the Smalltalk community who has no aversion to reusing the system's components. Users of the Smalltalk environment often spend as much time browsing the system classes to see whether there are classes which can be reused as they spend writing new classes. Software reuse in Smalltalk is prevalent because the Smalltalk language and environment are so special that it is easier to modify and reuse existing classes than to create new ones.

Nevertheless, reuse of software is not always straightforward in practice. In order to make reusability a reality under object-orientation, designers must create new reusable classes and easily find potentially reusable ones, already developed. Creating reusable classes is a complicated task because the class correctness becomes more critical since errors are replicated whenever and wherever a carelessly designed class is reused.

Finding existing classes easily means organizing them in such a way that they can be rapidly recovered when needed by designers. One real disadvantage of searching for classes in reusable libraries is the time that it takes to master large, and not always well organized, libraries of reusable classes. Traditionally, ways to overcome these complications have included attempts to provide written documentation for classes and to develop browsers that facilitate the selection and reuse of a class. Another major hindrance in creating a large reusable library is how to interconnect the complex semantic relationships which may exist between classes in an application domain. Therefore, there will always be a slow learning curve due to the inherent burden in understanding and relating the classes within a reusable library.

These difficulties often turn reusability into a superficial and haphazard process, and the usefulness of a reusable component depends more on the similarity of two applications, luck, and foresight of designers rather than on the engineering process. To achieve anything better than this *ad hoc* process, semantic relationships between reusable components need to be identified and kept in reusable libraries. A set of fixed relations which can be derived from the methodology for object-oriented design put forward in this book, and which can express links between components will be introduced later.

It should be emphasized that object-orientation is not a panacea for solving the problems regarding reuse of software. Reusability does not happen by chance and designers must plan to reuse old components, and new ones must be designed for reuse. Tools which facilitate the selection of potentially reusable components, as well as methodologies which encourage reusability are the keys to successful reuse of software components. Reusability should be enforced as part of a methodology that gives support for it through pragmatic steps that help find reusable components. By using the object-oriented methodology to be described in Chapter 3, reusability is taken into account during the design of a software system.

1.5.3. Software Life Cycle Models

Some important issues concerning software life cycle are considered from now on. It is appropriate to examine different software life cycle models in general and to point out their strong points and flaws before an alternative one is proposed. This discussion provides background for understanding the object-oriented software life cycle model introduced in Chapter 4.

Life cycle models for software production have long been used by software engineers. The primary utility of life cycle models is to identify and arrange the phases and stages involved in software development and evolution. They also accrue guidance to the sequence in which the major tasks to construct and maintain a software system should be performed.

Waterfall Software Life Cycle Model

The classic description of a software life cycle is based on a model commonly referred to as the *waterfall model* [37], which has become the most prevalent life cycle model. This model initially attempts to order phases within software development as a linear series of actions, each of which must be completed before the next is commenced. Although there are a variety of different names for each of the phases, they are basically identified as: requirements, specification, design, implementation and maintenance.

At a gross scale, four phases of the waterfall model are generally agreed upon: specification, design, implementation and maintenance. Often the requirements and specification phases are called analysis, therefore the analysis phase covers the time from the initiation of software development, through user needs and feasibility study, to the high level specification of the software system. Design can be divided into early design and detailed design; following from the design, implementation is carried out. During the maintenance phase, software engineers are asked to add new functionalities, fix faults, modify existing behaviour or enhance performance of an existing software.

The waterfall model is marked by the apparently neat, concise and logical ordering of the series of obvious phases that must be followed in order to create a software system. Such a model assumes that the specification phase must be completed and validated before design begins, and that the design phase must be completed and verified before implementation starts, and so on. Therefore, the waterfall model supposes that software engineers complete an entire step, before going to the next one.

Further revisions to this life cycle model consider that completion is seldom absolute and that iteration back to a previous stage is likely to happen. In an iterative waterfall model, if there is sufficient reason to do so, software engineers may return to a previously completed step, introduce a change, and then propagate the effects of that change forward in the software life cycle, as represented in Figure 1.6.

The waterfall model is frequently based on a view of the real-world application interpreted in terms of a functional decomposition. The idea is simple enough: select a piece of the application (initially the whole application) and determine its main parts, generally based on the required functionality for the software system. Repeat the

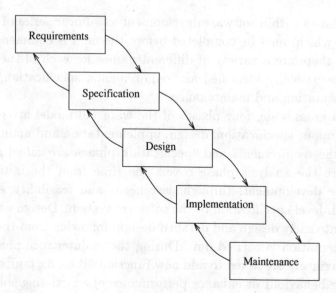

Figure 1.6: The classic waterfall software life cycle model

refinements on each of the subparts until they become well detailed. Functional decomposition is typically a top-down process and tools used to support this fashion, which is usually based on functions and data flow, include data flow diagram editors, structure chart editors, and data dictionary generators.

It is possible to categorize a functional decomposition approach as fundamentally top-down. A top-down tactic has the following characteristics:

- It progresses from the general to the specific.

- It decomposes software systems into layers and in each layer there is a uniform level of abstraction.

- Components at higher level of abstraction treat components at lower level as black boxes.

- Components at low level of abstraction are unaware of components at higher level of abstraction.

The top-down approach imposes some discipline to software development, but it has been criticized as not being totally appropriate to embrace contemporary software development paradigms, such as prototyping and object-orientation. However, despite the frequent criticism of the waterfall model, no satisfactory replacement has acquired widespread acceptance. The main flaws in the waterfall model can be summarized as follows:

- It takes no account of evolutionary development and prototyping.

- It often characterizes a software system as a single and large high level function.

- It is based on a functional decomposition strategy, and the data aspects are often neglected.

- It does not encourage reusability within its phases.

- It does not address the concern of developing similar software systems.

- It does not consider the previous knowledge that software engineers may have about the application domain.

- It assumes a deceitful uniform progression throughout software development.

- It attempts to separate software development into distinct phases, though it is quite common to carry out some of them in parallel.

The successive phases described in the waterfall model have helped eliminate many of the problems previously encountered during software development, therefore the model has gained great acceptability. But even after extensive revisions and refinements of the waterfall model, its basic scheme has encountered significant opposition, which has led to the formulation of substitute software life cycle models.

Spiral Software Life Cycle Model

An alternative software life cycle model, named *spiral model* [38], has been proposed mainly to speed up software development. A spiral model, as simply depicted in Figure 1.7, makes software development more flexible and it is strongly connected to prototyping. This is a process of creating a software prototype which exhibits some of the behaviour of the final software. Prototyping allows constructive feedback from potential users and designers, so that requirements can be refined and clarified early in the software development.

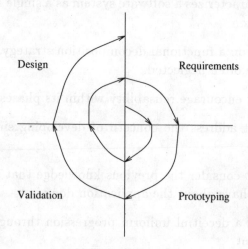

Figure 1.7: A spiral software life cycle model

A typical spiral model usually observes the following stages:

1. Identify the basic requirements and objectives of the application.

2. Study alternatives to implement a software system that meets these requirements.

3. Select one alternative that satisfies partial requirements.

4. Implement a prototype with a minimum effort in order to understand the overall nature of the software system.

5. Exercise and validate the prototype against the requirements and objectives, based on the experience from its use.

6. Use the feedback to understand better the design and requirements.

7. Go back to the first step.

The idea of producing, as early as possible, a working prototype is widely accepted in engineering. Similarly, the main idea behind this life cycle model is to build, cheaply and quickly, a prototype that partially meets known requirements for a software system, with a small team of designers. The purpose of a prototype is to construct an experimental sample, which is essentially a learning device and supplies feedback to designers, so that the final implemented version has a better chance of meeting the user requirements.

A big advantage that a prototype can bring to the requirements definition stage is the capability of bridging the communication gap which often exists between final users and designers because of their different background. The potential users experiment with the prototype for a period of time and supply feedback to designers concerning its strengths and weaknesses. Each cycle is completed with a validation and review of the prototype, and improvements added to the prototype until a complete software is built.

There are some advantages to this kind of incremental development:

- important feedback to designers is provided at the beginning of software development, when it is most needed and most useful;

- designers could make use of various prototypes, which allow them to evaluate and take a decision among several alternatives;

- many errors, non-viable and unattractive alternatives can be eliminated early;

- iterations and feedback are accommodated in the life cycle model;

- the software interface is defined and tested early;

- designers and users can see results much earlier in the development process, giving them a good psychological boost;

- costs are reduced because users do not suddenly change their requirements late in the development process.

A spiral model caters for an organized way to prototype and eventually to full software development. Besides, this model is beneficial in software development where many options are open, and requirements and constraints are unknown at the beginning. Evolutionary prototyping supports incremental development, so that a software system may be gradually developed and tested, allowing errors to be revealed and corrected earlier than in the waterfall model, which means that they are often cheaper to fix.

A prototype is neither intended to be complete nor supposed to be robust in the sense of a final piece of implemented software. Therefore, not all aspects of the software system are prototyped. Only the most important functionalities are emphasized, not the exceptional conditions nor particular special cases. Data validation and error handling are not as comprehensive in the prototype as they are in the final software system; performance considerations are frequently ignored too. Thus, a prototype is usually inefficient and clumsy because it has very limited error trapping and recovery procedures. Basically, the prototype is there to simply show, evolve and test an idea.

Because of these limitations, prototyping can be effective only as part of a disciplined software development. Without clear and explicit goals and a commitment to keep progress up to date, this process can degenerate into uncontrollable hacking. Consequently, rapid prototyping can be risky if it is decided to deliver the prototype as a product rather than discarding it. The construction of a prototype follows essentially a bottom-up fashion, which has the following characteristics:

- It surveys an application and attempts to identify necessary components.

- It gives priority to the discovery or modification of components over creation of new ones.

- It usually considers components as black-boxes.

- It assembles simple components to form larger and more complex ones.

- It progresses from the specific to the general.

Nevertheless, a bottom-up strategy is sometimes chaotic, and conservative designers might say that it is marked by a code-first-think-later mentality. Moreover, a purely bottom-up style is not appropriate for developing large software, thus, the smaller a software system is, the greater the likelihood that a bottom-up approach is successfully used.

Other Software Life Cycle Models

There is a significant change to the software life cycle as a result of the way in which object-orientation is applied to software development. As a consequence, designers have identified the need for a life cycle model that accounts for the iterative development and gradual changes which occur in the production of object-oriented software. However, only in the 1990s object-oriented software life cycle models have been introduced.

The *fountain model* [39] proposes a top-down analysis and a bottom-up implementation of object-oriented software. This is based on the recognition that the designer's view of a software system changes continuously, and software development is rarely well-behaved. The fountain model characterizes a software life cycle in terms of merging and overlapping the following activities: requirements analysis, user requirements specification, software requirements specification, system design, program design, coding, unit testing, system testing, program use and maintenance or further developments. Nevertheless, the fountain model does not state clearly, for example, when one activity finishes and another starts or what the deliverables of each stage should be. Indeed, this model is different from the waterfall model, in that, it acknowledges natural overlapping between two adjacent phases.

Booch [40] argues that it is not possible to categorize object-oriented design as a fundamentally top-down or bottom-up fashion, and proposes what is known as *"analyze a little, design a little and implement a little"* approach to software development. However, there are no systematic phases in this process and it seems to be a kind of design by trial and error offering an excuse for hacking. Such a tactic might be viewed as equivalent to a middle-out fashion. This line of thought makes it difficult to trace software development accurately because there is no delimited phases whatsoever.

Software life cycle models must provide a methodical framework for software development in such a way that progress can be effectively monitored with a provision of checkpoints and well-defined stages. Planning techniques should be efficiently applied and a library of reusable components could be extensively used. An alternative software life cycle model suitable for object-oriented software development and and evolution is put forward in Chapter 4.

1.6. Summary

This chapter has expanded on the background of the object-oriented paradigm. At first, it has introduced the notions of application domains and solution domains, and has showed how object-orientation brings these domains close together. After, the profile of current software has been characterized in terms of complexity, friendliness, extensibility and reusability. Then, the chapter has described the road towards object-oriented design and has presented an overview of well-known programming languages.

Furthermore, this chapter has investigated the main trends in the object-oriented arena and introduced concepts related to an object-oriented model (in particular for classes, objects and inheritance) in order to establish the terminology employed in this book. This has been necessary because there have been no generally accepted definitions of what these terms mean even though object-orientation has its roots back in the 1970s. The terminology is language independent and not linked with any object-oriented system. In fact, the proposed terminology has been used as way to characterize an object-oriented model, rather than give a precise definition of the paradigm.

Additionally, the chapter has presented essential background knowledge, and the philosophy upon which object-oriented design is based, by addressing questions such as: How can one design software systems entirely within an object-oriented fashion? How can one relate application domain, reusability and software life cycle models to object-oriented thinking? By addressing these issues, the most relevant features of object-oriented design have been characterized for use in subsequent chapters. It is important that an object-oriented design methodology be general enough to cover these issues.

In parallel with advances in object-oriented programming languages, several software development methodologies have been emerging, as well as tools which totally or partially automate such methodologies. In particular, various object-oriented methodologies have recently arisen to support software development based on object-orientation, as will be seen in the next chapter.

Exercises

1. What factors affect software complexity and why are large software systems difficult to develop?

2. What are the basic features of an object-oriented software?

3. Explain in your own words what the concepts of class, object and inheritance mean.

4. In which sense are the notions of classes and abstract data types connected?

5. Why modularity and encapsulation are important and how can they be accomplished under an object-oriented framework?

6. Write a class definition (including attributes and operations) for a stack.

7. Write a set of classes to manipulate graphical elements such as points, polygons and circles.

8. Write a set of classes for a software system that controls an elevator.

9. Draw a class hierarchy for a root *animal* class. Keep in mind that several solutions are possible, depending on the classification criteria.

10. Give three examples of class hierarchies where multiple inheritance naturally happens.

11. Discuss the advantages and drawbacks of single and multiple inheritance.

12. How can the notion of classes, objects, attributes and operations be emulated in procedural languages such as Pascal or C?

13. Why hardware seems to be more reusable than software?

14. Does programming language affect reuse?

15. Do software engineers prefer to built from scratch or to reuse software?

16. What is a software life cycle model?

17. Why the waterfall model is not a proper reflection of the activities involved in object-oriented software development?

18. What is a prototype? When is prototyping most convenient? Why prototypes should be eventually thrown away?

19. What features of object-oriented languages contribute to support rapid prototyping?

20. "Computing is basically simulation". Comment.

CHAPTER 2

OBJECT-ORIENTED METHODOLOGIES

This chapter presents the current state-of-the-art in object-oriented methodologies. The purpose of the first section is to identify the major similarities and differences between software development methodologies, and hence to compare and classify them. To a large extent, the classification and comparison synthesize different directions of thoughts, for instance, the phase of the software life cycle for which a methodology is suitable, if it is language-dependent, and whether it mixes with other approaches.

The second section gives a flavour of the most well-known object-oriented methodologies, so as to evaluate their main strengths and weaknesses. The coverage of these methodologies is concise and any graphical notation connected to each methodology is shown just briefly; the references at the end of the book provide additional information on them. Results from this survey are discussed in the last section.

It is useful at this point to explain concepts such as method, technique, methodology, tool and environment. A `method` is defined as a set of systematic activities to carry out a task. A `technique` is the way to execute activities recommended by methods, and a `methodology` is a set of methods and techniques with which an objective may be reached. A `tool` is a resource, automated or manual, which aids the application of a method or methodology; and finally, an `environment` is a collection of tools.

2.1. Classification of Methodologies

A wide range of methodologies for software development has been proposed over the last decades. Methodologies promote a fair discipline to handle the problem of software complexity because they usually offer a set of rules and guidelines to help software engineers understand, organize, decompose and represent software systems. Such methodologies may be classified into three groups. Firstly, some of them deal with functions; they emphasize refinement through functional decomposition. Typically, software development in this category follows a top-down fashion by successively refining functions, as with Structured Design [41] and Stepwise Refinement [42].

In a second trend, there are methodologies which recommend that software should be developed with emphasis on data rather than functions. To be more precise, the system architecture is based on the structure of the data to be processed by a software system. The system is structured mainly through the identification of data elements and their meaning. This sort of style is clearly visible in Jackson Structured Programming [43], and in the Entity-Relationship Model [44], which is the most common strategy to data modelling. This model offers a graphical notation easy to understand, yet powerful enough to model real-world applications, and entity-relationship diagrams are readily translated into a database implementation.

A third fashion consists of methodologies that aim to develop software from both functional and data points of view but separately. Examples of such methodologies are Structured Analysis and System

Specification [45], and Structured System Analysis [46]. As far as these methodologies are concerned, systems analysts can represent and refine functions through data flow diagrams and make use of a data dictionary to detail data. Such methodologies organize a specification and a design around hierarchies of functions. They both initially identify one or more high level functions which describe the overall purpose of the software system. Then, each high level function is decomposed into smaller, less complex functions, until they can be implemented.

There are also good examples of software development environments that automate some of those methodologies, such as PSL/PSA [47] and EPOS [48]. The chief purposes of these environments are to increase productivity and enhance the quality of the produced software.

A combination of tactics which follow a structured analysis, structured design and structured programming is collectively known as the `structured development` approach. Structured development iteratively divides complex functions into subfunctions. When the resulting subfunctions are simple enough, decomposition stops. This process of decomposition is known as the `functional decomposition` approach. Structured development also includes a variety of notations for representing software. During the specification and analysis phases, data flow diagrams, entity-relationship diagrams and a data dictionary are used to logically describe a software system. In the design phase, details are added to the specification model and the data flow diagrams are converted into structure chart diagrams ready to be implemented in a procedural language.

Preferably, there should be specific methodologies fitted to object-oriented software development because peculiar concepts are involved. The unsuitability of the above mentioned methodologies for tackling the object-oriented development complexity obliges software engineers to use two or three methodologies followed by an informal change of approaches, from functional decomposition to object-orientation, during software construction. For instance, the software engineer starts analysis following a functional decomposition point of view and afterwards, during the implementation phase, changes to an object-oriented fashion. This change in strategy leads the thought process to switch over to object-orientation in the middle of software development instead of starting putting classes, objects and inheritance to use from the outset.

Structured analysis has been suggested as an attractive front-end to object-oriented design primarily because it is well-known, many software engineers are trained in its techniques, and many tools support its notation. However, structured analysis is not the optimal front-end to object-oriented design, mainly because it can perpetuate a functional decomposition view of the real-world application. Applying functional decomposition first and object-orientation later in the same software development is likely to lead to trouble because functional decomposition cannot be properly mapped into object-oriented decomposition.

Object-orientation divides software into classes and establishes relationships between them. Objects model real-world entities and combine both attributes and operations. Each object is an instance of a class, which is the building block of the system architecture. A positive benefit of following object-oriented thinking is the traceability between software abstractions and reality because classes and objects map real-world entities into software components. Thus, any methodology which deals with object-thinking must have a means of expressing classes, objects and inheritance. Ideally, object-oriented analysis, design and implementation should be part of a software process in which an object-oriented philosophy is observed throughout software development, as illustrated in Figure 2.1. In this figure, the dashed arrows denote an unnatural mapping between concepts of different approaches as opposed to bold arrows.

Experience has shown that simply attempting to combine object-orientation with structured development is likely to give rise to future complications. It jeopardizes traceability from requirements to implementation as, in early phases, a software system is described in terms of functions and later on the description is changed to object-oriented concepts, as depicted in Figure 2.1. Furthermore, structured development methodologies do not place information around objects but on data flow between functions, and a software system is composed of data flow and functions. In contrast, object-orientation organizes a software system around classes and objects which exist in the designer's mind.

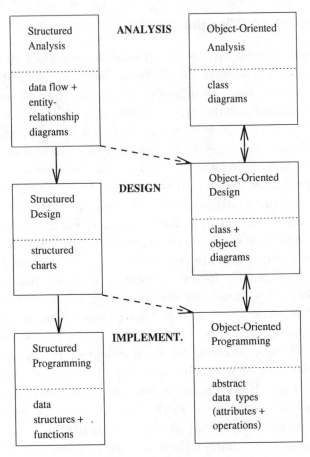

Figure 2.1: Some combinations of approaches

Moreover, since the notions of class, object and inheritance are fundamental to object-orientation, if a software system is designed following this fashion, an object-oriented language should be used in the implementation phase. Of course, there are attempts to implement ideas without a language that directly supports them, but the results are not likely to be as good as using a suitable programming language.

From the Designer's Viewpoint

Designers who have a strong background in object-oriented programming naturally possesses ample perception of object-oriented concepts and have almost no difficulty in figuring out classes and objects. These designers have written code using an object-oriented language but are often unable to separate design from implementation. Few of them even suggest that methods are unnecessary, and that object-orientation obviates the need for methodologies.

A second trend is embodied by designers who have considerable experience with structured development methodologies. These designers have strong background on data flow diagrams, entity-relationship diagrams and structure charts; they argue that structured development and object-orientation are correlative. These designers have a good grasp of traditional software engineering methods and tend to freely mix concepts from a number of different techniques with object-oriented thinking. Actually, they have not changed their mindset to embrace the object-oriented technology. They believe that structured development and object-thinking are complementary rather than opposing strategies and each can be applicable to different stages of software production. However, these designers have come to realize that those traditional structured methodologies based on functional decomposition do not take the advantages of inheritance.

Another tendency is characterized by those designers with substantial understanding of both object-oriented techniques and software engineering principles. Such designers have attempted to come up with fresh ideas and bring them into synchronization with object-orientation. They believe that object-orientation is so unique that designers basically have to think again over traditional ideas of the past and tackle object-oriented software development with a clean slate; this textbook supports such a trend.

2.1.1. Classification of Existing Object-Oriented Methodologies

The state-of-the-art of object-oriented methodologies is evolving rapidly. There has been a profusion of methods for analysis and design influenced by a variety of different backgrounds [49]. As the methodologies mature, they are likely to incorporate ideas from one another. Nevertheless, it can be noticed that there are two major directions in the development of object-oriented methodologies:

1. **Adaptation:** this is concerned with the mixing of object-orientation with well-known structured development methodologies.

2. **Assimilation:** this emphasizes the importance of an object-oriented approach for developing software, but following the traditional waterfall software life cycle model.

Adaptation

Adaptation proposes a framework for mixing object-orientation with existing methodologies. It has been suggested that a combination of structured development with object-thinking helps tackle the problem of software construction. Designers apply their experience and intuition to derive a specification from an informal description in order to get high level abstractions for the system, relying on functional decomposition. The adaptation of structured development to object-orientation preserves the specification and analysis phases using data flow diagrams and devises heuristics to convert these diagrams into an object model in such way that subsequent phases can then follow an object-oriented fashion. The advantages of such an adaptive strategy are:

- A complementary (though unnatural) coupling between structured development and object-orientation.

- Structured development methodologies are widely known and used, and follow a top-down functional decomposition, the most common trend for software development.

- A smoother migration from an old, practiced and well-known approach to a new one including classes, objects and inheritance.

- A gradual change of tools and environments.

Currently, the most widely used software engineering methodologies are still those for structured development. Such methodologies are popular because they are applicable to many types of application domains. On account of this popularity, structured development has been combined with object-orientation. Therefore, designers who come from traditional software engineering background, with sufficient experience in functional decomposition and data modelling techniques, will probably find the methodologies Object-Oriented Analysis [50] and Object-Oriented Systems Analysis [51] familiar as they are clearly adaptations of traditional structured development and data modelling techniques. These methodologies may be employed during a period of transition from structured development to object-orientation as a compromise. However, they cannot allow the full advantages of object-oriented thinking to be gained.

This tendency can also be seen in the early version of Object-Oriented Development [52] and its successors, such as General Object-Oriented Development [53], Hierarchical Object-Oriented Design [54], Jalote [55] and Object-Oriented Structured Design [56]. These methodologies do not make an adequate distinction between definition of classes and use of objects, which is essential for the exploitation of the object-oriented paradigm. Similarly, they have offered limited support for inheritance of commonalities in a hierarchy of classes; they tend to be oriented to Ada notations of *package* and *task*, rather than to more general notions of object-oriented design.

Other less known proposals where object-oriented concepts are by-products of structured development can be mentioned. Some of these methods are merely extensions of structured development methodologies. Masiero and Germano [57] and Hull [58] put together object-orientation and Jackson System Development [59], and the design is implemented in Ada. Bailin [60] and Bulman [61] mix up object-orientation with Structured System Analysis [46] and the Entity-Relationship Model [44] in an object-oriented requirements specification model. Lastly, Alabiso [62] and Ward [63] combine object-thinking with Structured Analysis and System Specification [45] and Structured Design [41] to face analysis and design.

Adaptation approaches are trying to evolve object-oriented methods from traditional structured ones and as a result bringing their limitations into. More importantly, they are not fitted to object-oriented development as inheritance is not fully exploited.

Assimilation

Assimilation is a trend that puts object-orientation into the classic waterfall model. In recent years several truly object-oriented methodologies have emerged but they partially cover the software life cycle. Several authors have tried to place object-orientation into this framework: Object-Oriented Analysis and Design [40], Responsibility-Driven Design [64], Object Modeling Technique [65], and Objectory [66] can be considered as good representatives of such a trend.

So far these methodologies are not generally accepted, but their main ideas encompass object-thinking as they at least rely on classes, objects and inheritance. Some of these methodologies still need to be applied to developing large scale software to be practically evaluated and further improved.

2.2. Survey of Existing Methodologies

When unimportant or trivial software must be created, there is no need to consider software development methodologies. Designers log on to their computers and immediately start writing their programs; a lot of programs have been written in such a way. This form of development is feasible if a few designers work on a small project, but it is not proper when serious software systems have to be built. In the latter case, the use of methodologies is highly recommendable because they help structure the software as a whole, and standardize its construction.

As software is essentially abstract, it becomes difficult to be represented. In fact, there are many kinds of software, for instance, real-time, process-control, scientific and commercial systems, which require varied supporting methodologies. Since the application domains are different, methodologies with specific characteristics should be employed. Moreover, there are some methodologies which are only applied to certain phases of the software life cycle. Such restrictions are manifested in the absence of one methodology for software production that is widely accepted and used. As a result there are a number of methodologies, methods and techniques, different notations and conflicting rules, each with its own advantages and disadvantages, as can be seen in the next subsections.

2.2.1. Booch Methodologies and Influences

The history of object-oriented technology dates back from the 1970s, but until the mid-1980s, much of the work in this field focused on object-oriented programming. The application of object-oriented thinking to software design has probably occurred since that time, mainly by designers familiar with Simula. From the beginning of the 1980s, some attempts to develop software systems using object-orientation have emerged. The first significant step towards an object-oriented design methodology started within the Ada community. Many ideas about object-oriented design came out with the works of Abbott [67] and Booch [68].

Booch set out to find some techniques to introduce software engineering principles into the Ada training effort and identified the work of Abbott as relevant. Abbott had proposed a simple methodology to design using nouns and verbs. Booch systematized that methodology, and referred to it as object-oriented design. Both Abbott and Booch have preached that a design should start with an informal textual description of the real-world application and from this description designers could clear up objects. Booch's idea is significant because it was one of the earliest object-oriented design methodologies to appear in the literature, and Booch himself has become one of the most influential advocates of object-oriented technology.

As far as Booch's influences are concerned, they can be summarized as follows: what has come to be known as object-oriented design within the Ada community was first put forward as Object-Oriented Design [68], after extended to Object-Oriented Development [52], and later refined by General Object-Oriented Development [53], Hierarchical Object-Oriented Design [54], Jalote [55] and Object-Oriented Structured Design [56]. These methodologies concentrate on identifying objects and operations, and are object-oriented in the sense that they view a software system as a set of objects. Most of them rely on an informal description of the software requirements, from where objects, attributes and operations are identified. Moreover, they apply hierarchical decomposition, a trend to decompose a system by breaking it into subparts through a series of top-down refinements.

Abbott Methodology

Abbott [67] methodology is based upon the description of a real-world application using natural language, and deriving a design by examining mainly nouns and verbs in that description. Abbott believes that the essential ideas of the application should be stated in sentences with which designers work in order to understand the features of the application. The methodology consists of three steps:

1. Develop colloquial and general statements for the application. This informal description, which states the application domain and the application itself, should be expressed in application domain vocabulary. In other words, write straightforward natural

language paragraphs which portray the application within its application domain.

2. Formalize the casual description. The formalization consists of identifying data types, objects, operations and control structures by looking at the natural language words and phrases in the informal description. The formalization substeps are:

   (a) Pick out the data types. Common nouns and noun phrases are good candidates.

   (b) Identify the objects for these data types. A proper noun or direct reference suggests an object.

   (c) Work out the operations to be applied to these objects. This can be done by examining verbs and predicates.

   (d) Organize the operations into the control structures implied in a straightforward way by the informal description.

3. Segregate the solution in two parts: packages and subprograms. The packages contain the formalization of the application domain, in other words, the data types (objects) and their operations. The subprograms contain the steps (expressed in terms of the data types and operations defined in the packages) to simulate that particular application.

The steps focus on what must be done to solve a problem and then how a solution can be accomplished. The level of abstraction is very high before step 3 is reached. In simple terms, the main idea is to pick out all nouns and verbs in a narrative specification. Objects in the design are derived from nouns, and operations are inferred from verbs. Obviously, some judgment must be applied to disregard irrelevant nouns and verbs and to translate the remaining concepts into a proper design. Adjectives and adverbs become attributes and operations respectively. Since an attribute helps discern peculiar characteristics of an object, it can be used to establish the constraints of the software.

It should be noticed that although these steps may look mechanical, they are not an automatic procedure. It is not just a matter of examining the syntax of a natural language description. The process of identifying the data types, objects, operations and control structures from a given narrative description requires a great deal of knowledge about the application domain as well as an intuitive understanding of the application.

Several observations can be made at this point. Firstly, Abbott ignores inheritance while the steps are carried out. Secondly, the viability of the technique of creating a narrative explanation of a problem, and then selecting data types, objects, attributes and operations for a software system from nouns, verbs, adjectives and adverbs of that informal description is doubtful. It inherently lacks rigour due to the impreciseness of natural languages. Thirdly, methodologies which rely on verbose descriptions are useful to make small projects where conceptual links are minimal, but not to design sizeable software due to the ambiguity of natural languages and the lack of standard structures. Finally, when a software system is large and complex with many interacting components, it is very difficult to produce a precise, concise and at the same time complete narrative description. Therefore, the suitability of Abbott methodology for developing substantial software is questionable.

Booch Methodologies

Booch [68] has also viewed the technique of picking out nouns and verbs as one out of many that could help identify objects. However, realizing its setbacks and recognizing that such a strategy actually had never been intended for producing large software systems, he has not advised the use of a narrative description anymore. Instead, Booch has combined object-oriented design with existing methodologies and called it Object-Oriented Development [52], which suggests that Structured System Analysis [46] or Jackson System Development [59] can be used during the requirements and specification phases as a step before object-oriented design.

This methodology begins with a data-flow-diagram-based specification, decomposes that into objects, finds dependencies between objects, and maps the design into Ada statements. During this process, inheritance is deemed important but not essential, and software development without inheritance is still considered object-oriented. This methodology divides the design process into the following steps:

1. Define the problem, even informally.

2. Devise a specification.

3. Identify the objects and their attributes from the specification.

4. Identify the operations provided by and required of each object.

5. Establish the visibility of each object in relation to other objects.

6. Establish the interface of each object.

7. Implement the objects.

Booch defines an object as an entity that:

- has a state;

- is denoted by a name;

- is an instance of some class;

- has restricted visibility of and by other objects;

- is characterized by actions it provides and requires of other objects.

While the identification of objects is performed, objects with similar properties should establish a class, so a few classes appear early in the design process. This methodology uses a graphical representation for a class which is helpful to visualize the architecture of the system. Such a representation is based on a box consisting of an externally visible part that symbolizes a type and its operations, along with a private part utilized to describe implementation details. The boxes constitute diagrams that show interdependencies among objects through arrows, as illustrated in Figure 2.2.

The implementation of a class is carried out in Ada. The transformation of a design detailed by the graphical notation is forthright; each class represented by a box is translated into a package in Ada. A package is made up of two parts: a specification denoting the data types that can be used externally, and a body describing the implementation of the operations.

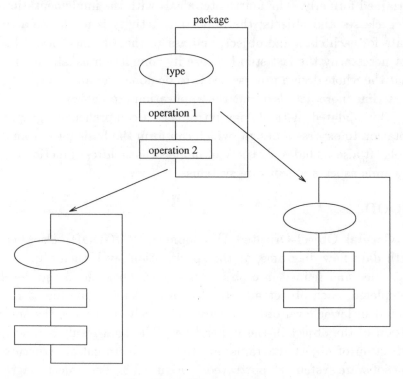

Figure 2.2: Classes as packages

Object-Oriented Analysis and Design [40] is an upgraded version of Object-Oriented Development [52], however, this new version conveys the impression that it is no longer Ada-oriented. The first step entails the identification of classes and objects at a high level of abstraction;

at that level, the fundamental task is the discovery of key abstractions in the application. The second step involves the definition of the semantics of these classes and objects; here, designers must act as detached outsiders, viewing each class from the perspective of its interface.

The third step requires the creation of relationships among these classes and objects; this step establishes how objects interact within the system, with regard to the semantics of the key abstractions determined formerly. The fourth step deals with the implementation of such classes and objects; the important activity is to choose a template for each class and object, and assign them to modules. This is not necessarily the last step because its completion usually demands that the whole design process needs to be done over and over, but the next time more details about the application are known.

This updated methodology introduces a comprehensive graphical notation to express a design, which can form the basis for automated tools. It also includes a variety of models that address functional and dynamic aspects of software systems.

GOOD

General Object-Oriented Development [53] (GOOD) also begins with data flow diagrams, at the specification level, then objects are identified and refined into object diagrams. Once the design level is completed, each object may be decomposed into sub-objects represented in lower level object diagrams conceived to meet the specification of the object in the upper level. The final result is a layered collection of object diagrams outlining the hierarchical structure of the software system, as portrayed in Figure 2.3. The object diagrams depict control flow and module dependencies between objects. At the lowest level, objects are completely decomposed into procedures along with their internal data structures.

A seniority hierarchy is expressed by the topology of connections in object diagrams. Each object is a node of a graph, and if object A somehow invokes any operation of object B, then there is an arrow from A to B. Any layer in the seniority hierarchy can call on any operation in an equivalent or lower level layer, but never any operation in a higher level layer. Thus, all cyclic links between objects must be contained within the same layer in the seniority hierarchy.

GOOD provides an object description which includes a list of all operations offered by the object, and for each outgoing arrow, the operations required by that object. This methodology is similar in many ways to functional decomposition. At the lowest level, objects are totally decomposed into low level objects, then each primitive object is implemented in Ada.

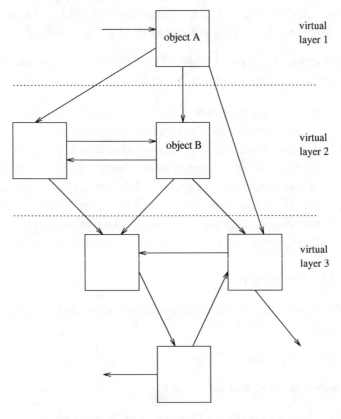

Figure 2.3: Seniority hierarchy in object diagrams

HOOD

Hierarchical Object-Oriented Design [54] (HOOD) is an Ada-based methodology too, that is, with Ada as the target programming language. HOOD has been developed by taking as its starting point the ideas from Booch's early work, as can be clearly seen from the steps below. This methodology proposes four stages to software design:

1. Definition and analysis of the real-world application.

2. Design a solution using a natural language description.

3. Selection of nouns to make a list of objects, and verbs to set up a list of operations. This is labeled the Informal Solution Strategy.

4. Production of a formal Object Description Skeleton which is used to generate source code in Ada.

A HOOD tool supports the third stage by creating lists of words to be objects or operations. The objects and operations are then combined into a table from which object diagrams can be created. These diagrams outline the behaviour of the objects. There is another tool to deal with the generation of code in Ada from the Object Description Skeleton that contains formal specifications of the operations. Although the design process is based on the encapsulation of data and procedures by means of objects, inheritance is not fully assisted.

Jalote Methodology

Jalote [55] puts forward a design methodology that comprises three main steps:

1. Define the problem.

2. Develop an informal strategy.

3. Formalize the strategy. This step has four substeps:

   (a) identify objects and their attributes;

(b) figure out the operations on the objects;

(c) establish the interfaces of the objects;

(d) implement the objects.

The objective of the first step is to properly understand the nature of the problem. In the second step an informal strategy to solve the problem is stated using natural language descriptions. In the third step, the objects are initially identified from the informal strategy, then the operations on the objects are cleared up. The interfaces of the objects are established by clarifying the visibility of each object.

Jalote introduces two concepts named *functional refinement stages* and *nested objects*. In the functional refinement stages, extra operations are identified and further refined. By the time these refinements finish, the algorithms needed to solve the original problem will have been detailed to a satisfactory level. To refine an object, informal descriptions of all operations defined on the object are written. Further, embedded objects (denominated nested objects) required to implement the operations come out. This step ends when objects are simple enough to be promptly implemented in Ada.

By introducing the concepts of functional refinement stages and nested objects, this methodology incorporates a top-down fashion into object-oriented design. Nevertheless, the methodology focuses exclusively on a systematic process to derive design and implementation towards Ada; it does not propose any graphical notation to represent the design.

OOSD

Object-Oriented Structured Design [56] (OOSD) promotes ideas of both structured and object-oriented design. Therefore, it allows designers to gradually shift from structured development to object-orientation. OOSD also incorporates the concept of monitors for concurrent programming along with other important features:

- It supports class hierarchy and inheritance.

- It is independent of any programming language.

- It offers a formal grammar for a textual description of a design.

- It has a mechanism to depict exceptional conditions.

- It assists in a wide variety of software systems, including both sequential and concurrent models of execution.

This methodology enforces a graphical notation for design. In general terms, OOSD represents a class with a rectangle and employs overlapping small boxes to symbolize operations. An operation overlapping a class rectangle suggests a visible part of that class. Besides, an operation can be placed completely inside a class rectangle to indicate that the operation is hidden from other classes. OOSD borrows the parameter passing notation from Structured Design [41], where arrows indicate the kind of parameters (e.g. data or control). Exceptions are drawn as diamonds overlapping a class rectangle anywhere around its perimeter (see Figure 2.4). After defining a class, designers can instantiate its objects. However, OOSD regards this step as a matter of implementation since instantiation is connected to the use of a class not to its definition. Inheritance is depicted by a hierarchy of class rectangles linked by dashed arrows.

It is evident that OOSD mixes up object-oriented concepts with structured development principles as the convention for parameter passing comes from Structured Design. Additionally, it follows a top-down functional decomposition into modules, ending up with Ada as an implicitly suggested implementation language, thereby accommodating two important design philosophies. However, it does not set up guidelines to work out classes and operations, so it is supposed that designers should follow steps recommended by other methodologies.

OOSD concentrates mainly on a graphical representation without addressing the method by which a design is created and gives no explicit tactic for diagramming software decomposition, necessary for large projects. Although OOSD delineates relationships between

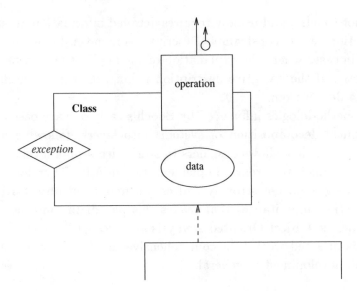

Figure 2.4: Class representation in OOSD

classes, it does not show detailed interactions between objects. It is expected that designers will bring their own methods into OOSD, which simply offers a notation for object-oriented design, not a step-by-step methodology.

Comments on Booch Methodologies and Influences

Biased by Booch's original ideas, several design methodologies combining object-orientation with other well-known techniques have emerged, as has been briefly explained above. Nevertheless, methodologies based on verbose descriptions have many shortcomings due to the informality and ambiguity inherent in the use of natural languages.

As an illustration, what exactly does the phrase "get a course from a course list and assign the course a room number in a building" mean? It is not enough to rely on normal usage of these terms; a more appropriate explanation is needed to come up with a design. In fact, the writing of a complete narrative description is neither straightforward nor concise, and usually requires detailed information about the application and its constraints. Descriptions in natural language work better in cases where the explanation of the application can be given succinctly. If the narrative description is long, it becomes useless to derive a design from.

All methodologies influenced by Booch's early one are based upon hierarchical decomposition of systems into layers, following a top-down fashion that allows designers to start with a high level abstraction and refine it towards an implementation in Ada. Therefore, those methodologies do not strongly address an important object-oriented concept (i.e. inheritance) that makes this paradigm more powerful. Nevertheless, Object-Oriented Analysis and Design [40] extends previous Ada-oriented work to a comprehensive methodology for object-oriented development in general.

2.2.2. Responsibility-Driven Design

Responsibility-Driven Design [64] focuses on the identification of responsibilities and contracts to build a design model. *Responsibility* is a way to apportion work among a group of objects comprising an application. A *contract* is a set of related responsibilities characterized by object interactions, and describes how a given client object interacts with a server object.

This methodology emphasizes the actions that must be accomplished and which objects will perform these actions. The responsibilities of an object are the services it provides for all objects with which it communicates. In an interaction between two objects, both must comply with a contract: the client object by making the requests the contract specifies, and the server object by responding appropriately to such requests. Objects fulfil their responsibilities either by performing the necessary computation themselves or by collaborating with other objects. The responsibility-driven design recommends the following steps to design a software system:

1. Select noun phrases from the specification and build a list of nouns. Identify candidate classes from noun phrases by modelling

physical and conceptual entities in the application. Then, pick out candidates for high level classes by grouping entities that share common properties, and write a short statement of the purpose of each class on a *class card* used to capture information about a class.

2. The design continues by defining the objective of each class and the role it will play in the system in terms of responsibilities, including the state that a class keeps and the actions that a class offers. When responsibilities are assigned to a class, every instance of that class naturally has these responsibilities. Therefore, responsibilities are meant to convey the services an object contributes to and its place in the system. The responsibilities are found by recalling the purpose of each class in terms of the actions that its objects cater for. This step considers the use of inheritance as a means of grouping common responsibilities as high as possible in class hierarchies, so that the `is-a` relationship between classes is valid. Services defined by a class include those listed on the class card, plus the responsibilities inherited from its superclasses.

3. In the third step, subsystems are recognized. A subsystem is a set of classes (and possibly other subsystems) collaborating to meet a common set of responsibilities (contracts). From the outside, a subsystem can be viewed as a collection of classes which supplies clearly delimited services. In order to work out possible subsystems, designers should look for collaborations that happen frequently. Collaborations represent an exchange of messages from one object to another in fulfillment of a contract. Classes in a subsystem should collaborate to support a cohesive set of responsibilities, should be strongly interdependent, and the subsystem division should minimize the number of collaborations a class has with other classes or subsystems. The methodology also recommends going back to earlier stages to refine the responsibilities, contracts, classes and subsystems.

As the steps are followed, the responsibility-driven methodology considers walk-throughs to explore design possibilities and to record the result of a design on class cards. Such cards form a simple technique for teaching object-oriented thinking to newcomers. Each class card contains the name of a class, a description of the responsibilities associated with that class and its collaborators. They record subclass and superclass relationships as well. Each candidate class is written on a class card, as outlined in Figure 2.5, its superclasses and subclasses are described in the lines below the class name. Each identified responsibility is succinctly written on the left side of the card. If collaborations are required to fulfil a responsibility, the name of each class that supplies the necessary services is written on the right of the responsibility.

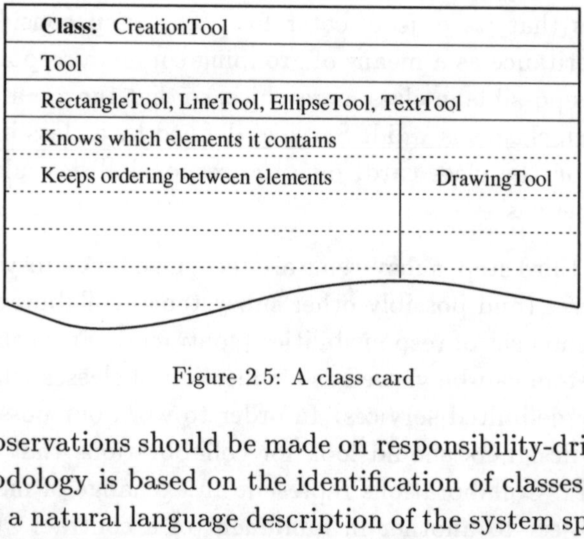

Class: CreationTool	
Tool	
RectangleTool, LineTool, EllipseTool, TextTool	
Knows which elements it contains	
Keeps ordering between elements	DrawingTool

Figure 2.5: A class card

Some observations should be made on responsibility-driven design. This methodology is based on the identification of classes by looking at nouns in a natural language description of the system specification. Such a tactic has the same drawbacks as the first versions of Abbott and Booch methodologies, pointed out at the end of last section. The methodology also suggests the use of class cards to detail classes and subsystems. This technique works well with simple software but its applicability to design large and complex software is doubtful, as the number of classes and subsystems grows sharply, the number and arrangements of class cards may become cumbersome and difficult to manage.

Additionally, responsibility-driven design bases inheritance merely on responsibilities, and ignores inheritance of attributes. Besides, the methodology splits a large system into subsystems only after identifying some classes and their responsibilities. However, the partitioning into subsystems should also be discussed at the beginning of software development as a scheme to decompose large software.

2.2.3. OOA

The main steps established by Object-Oriented Analysis [50] (OOA) can be briefly described as:

- Identify objects.

- Identify structures.

- Identify subjects.

- Define attributes.

- Define services.

Identification of objects encompasses the understanding of the application as well as finding abstractions of data and processing on this data. At first, designers have to concentrate on the application domain and look for entities, devices, events, roles played and organizational units in order to comprehend needed behaviour, requested services and essential requirements; at the end of this stage, objects are identified.

Identification of structures aims at managing the complexity of the application by constructing a hierarchy based on specialization and generalization of objects; and assembling objects by aggregation and decomposition, in order to reflect the partial and the whole software system. Subjects provide a mechanism for controlling how much of the system a designer is able to consider at a time. They are connected to the structures identified in the previous step. Thus, subjects divide the software into partitions composed of structures; when grouped together, correlated subjects characterize a subsystem.

Attributes are seen as data elements used to limit the meaning of objects. Definition of attributes involves examining the application domain, and attaching individual data elements or collections of related data elements to certain entities and then to objects associated with these entities. A service is the processing performed upon receipt of a message. The central issue in defining services is to figure out the required behaviour of each object; a secondary issue is to arrange the necessary communication between objects. OOA introduces a graphical notation for objects too, as illustrated in Figure 2.6.

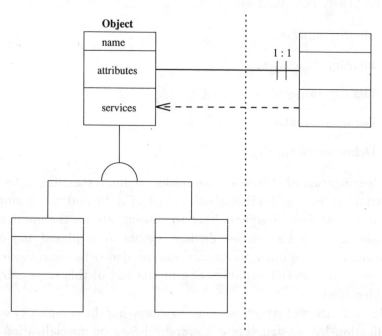

Figure 2.6: Object representation in OOA

Basically, an object is represented individually by a rectangle containing its name, attributes and services. Specialization is denoted by lines with semi-circles at the end of the objects. Subjects are separated by dotted lines. Relationships between objects can be 1:1 or N:M. Finally, messages are indicated by dashed lines linking the involved objects.

This methodology oversimplifies the object-oriented paradigm by combining the concepts of classes and objects, during the analysis phase, as simply objects. Throughout the methodology, these concepts are never separated. Basically, OOA concentrates on modelling real-world entities as objects, and it can be viewed as an extension of the Entity-Relationship Model, implying that it is an incremental improvement over an existing technique for data modelling. OOA also suggests the use of ordinary 3" by 5" index cards as a substitute for software tools; this is a trivialization of the benefits of using computer-aided tools. Moreover, the impact of this methodology on other phases of the software life cycle has not been discussed.

2.2.4. OMT

Object Modeling Technique [65] (OMT) makes use of object and data modelling as a basis for software development. Fundamentally, OMT proposes three models:

- The *object model* describes the features of a software system in terms of classes, in an object model diagram. The object model is represented by graphs whose nodes are classes and arcs denote relationships of specialization, composition, or any other connection between classes (see Figure 2.7).

- The *dynamic model* details the aspects of a system that change over time due to events, and it is used to understand the software control flow. The dynamic model is conveyed by familiar state transition diagrams whose nodes are states and arcs are transitions (triggered by events) between states.

- The *functional model* reports the data transformations within the software and employs the well-known data flow diagrams to express the computation of output values from input values.

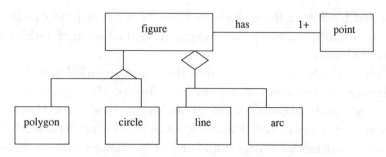

Figure 2.7: An object model diagram

OMT recommends three stages to produce a design:

1. The *analysis stage* captures meaningful properties of a real-world application and uses the object, dynamic and functional models to represent these properties. The purpose of this stage is to understand the application in terms of classes.

2. The *system design stage* focuses on decisions concerning the high level architecture of a software system. In this stage the system is divided into subsystems, and object-thinking is not employed.

3. The *object design stage* targets at the data structures and algorithms necessary to implement each class in the object model. During this stage, dynamic and functional aspects are combined and then refined, as a consequence, further details about the control flow are understood.

Some considerations on OMT can be made at this point. The first stage of OMT is equivalent to OOA, in that, it basically models the application in terms of classes and special relationships between them. However, it is confusing that the object model actually deals with classes. Later, during the system design and object design stages, OMT incorporates structured development based on a functional decomposition strategy following the traditional waterfall cycle.

2.2.5. OOSA

Object-Oriented Systems Analysis [51] (OOSA) is an analysis methodology with an associated graphical notation, which is based on a variation of the Entity-Relationship Model combined with Structured System Analysis. The notation can be applied to describe objects, attributes and relationships, where a relationship indicates any link between objects. OOSA suggests that designers should construct three models:

- The information model.

- The state model.

- The process model.

The information model expresses objects, attributes and relationships in an *information structure diagram*, as can be seen in Figure 2.8. The state model expands the information model by embodying the behaviour of each object using a standard state transition diagram. The process model comprises data flow diagrams including states and transitions from the state model.

Figure 2.8: An information structure diagram

OOSA offers a data modelling technique and embraces the concept of an object as a record in a relational database. Nevertheless, OOSA fails to account for the vast majority of object-oriented ideas and an ordinary graphical notation is prescribed for object-oriented system analysis. Indeed, the graphical notation is taken primarily from entity-relationship diagrams and data flow diagrams found in others structured methods. In various aspects, OOSA is similar to OOA. Both methodologies have in common the emphasis on data modelling as the chief task to be performed during software development.

2.2.6. OSA

Object-Oriented Systems Analysis [69] (OSA) introduces an analysis method that purposefully contains no design features. It avoids being a preliminary design method as it specifically omits several design aspects claimed to aid implementation but to hinder analysis. In addition to being a carefully crafted analysis method, OSA is also executable. Each modelling component has a formal syntax and semantics to simulate execution even during systems analysis.

OSA provides an extensive graphical notation to produce an analysis model comprising three integrated submodels:

- The *object-relationship model* for representing objects and their relationships to other objects.

- The *object-behaviour model* for expressing objects' behaviour from their creation to destruction, including concurrent and serial, deterministic and non-deterministic, as well as normal and exceptional behaviour.

- The *object-interaction model* for depicting interactions among objects, such as message passing, information exchange and action triggering.

Although it is object-oriented, OSA is not encapsulation-oriented, in which everything must be packed into a class describing an object as a set of attributes and operations. Instead, it simply uses an object point of view to guide systems analyst to study, document and understand the application. There is no classes and the system analyst identifies all "things" as objects, then work out relationships among them. In fact, this is a weak point about OSA because it is of paramount importance to distinguish classes from objects.

2.2.7. Objectory

Objectory [66] is claimed to be a full object-oriented development methodology. It combines a technique to develop large software, called *block design*, along with *conceptual modelling* and object-orientation. The methodology states that it is quite natural to unite these three approaches since they rely on similar ideas aiming at, among other things, the production of reusable software components. Conceptual modelling emphasizes finding abstractions suitable to model a real-world application, and it is appropriate for representing the entities of the application as well as the relationships between such entities.

Objectory concerns the design of large scale software systems that have been developed today using structured methods. The base of the methodology is a design technique denominated the block design, which is now widespread within the telecommunications industry. Block design can be seen as assembling a collection of properly interconnected blocks and components, each one symbolizing a packaged service, as sketched in Figure 2.9. The software is viewed as a

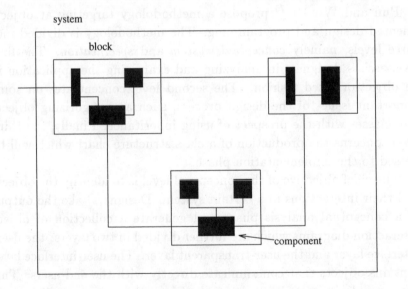

Figure 2.9: An objectory system

group of linked blocks and components selected in a top-down fashion. In a simplified way, the software is built from groups of reusable blocks. The block itself is composed of lower level reusable components, which are standard modules that can be reused in many different software systems. Reusable blocks and components are implemented as classes using an object-oriented programming language.

The scenario that Objectory assumes for building up a software system is similar to the manner in which production is carried out in many other engineering disciplines such as house construction or the design of electronic systems. The main criticism that can be made about Objectory concerns the fact that it mixes up different techniques, thus it is not purely object-oriented. Furthermore, the niche where this methodology excels is telecommunications systems as block design was created to address software production in that application domain.

2.2.8. Pun and Winder Methodology

Pun and Winder [70] propose a methodology targeting at object-oriented design and programming. The methodology is divided into three levels, namely conceptual, system and specification. The first level assists designers in analyzing and examining the application in an object-oriented fashion. The second level concentrates on some important issues of the design process, such as categorizing objects into classes with the prospect of using inheritance. Finally, the third level concerns the production of a class structure chart which will be passed to the implementation phase.

The chief objective of the conceptual level is to identify the objects and their interactions in a certain system. Designers take the output of a conceptual analysis phase and generate a collection of object interaction diagrams which are further divided in two layers: the user-interface layer and the user-transparent layer. The user-interface layer contains objects that communicate directly with the end-users. This layer supplies a visual presentation of how the software will look to its end-users; menus and forms are picked out as typical interfacing objects.

The user-transparent layer comprises specific software objects that are invisible to end-users who need not to be aware of the existence of such objects. Only designers know exactly what these objects are. The separation of the conceptual level into two layers highlights the importance of user interface design early in software development. Object interaction diagrams are the documentation of the objects and interactions found in the software. Thus, at the end of the conceptual level, a list of objects and operations will have been created.

After being identified, such objects have to be built. The system level is where the construction of each individual object takes place. In this process, every object has to be an instance of some class. If there is no suitable class for an object, designers have to make up a new one. So, at this point, designers must search and get to know the available classes. The new class may be a completely separate one or it can be placed either as a subclass or superclass of existing classes. Thus, the creation of extra classes may involve the use of inheritance.

The specification level mainly guides designers to start up the implementation. With the information obtained from the conceptual and system levels, designers can choose crucial objects and their interactions. These interactions are depicted in class structure charts. The aims of class structure charts are to clearly express class hierarchical structures as well as lay out their operations and messages.

2.2.9. JSD

Jackson System Development [59] (JSD) does not distinguish between analysis and design, instead it lumps both phases together under specification. The methodology begins by examining the real-world application and first determines the *what-to-do* and then the *how-to-do*. This methodology is intended especially for real-world applications in which timing plays a key role. A *specification model* describes the application in terms of entities, actions and ordering of actions. JSD also accepts that entities usually come out as nouns in requirements statements and actions emerge from verbs in that description.

JSD has some features which may appear on the surface to be related to object-orientation. The main task is to model the real-world application and to identify *entities* (which could be viewed as objects), *actions* (i.e. operations) and their interactions. However, JSD is not fully suitable for object-oriented design because there is little in it to support object-orientation, for instance, the notion of inheritance is entirely missing.

2.2.10. Graphical Notations for Implementation

Cunningham and Beck [71] propose diagrams for representing Smalltalk programs. In the diagrams, objects are indicated by boxes, as drawn in Figure 2.10. Each box is labeled with a class name and possibly its superclass. The diagrams also emphasize the message passing that takes place between objects. When one object invokes a method upon another object through a message, that message is shown as an arc originating in the sending object and landing in the receiving object. The various computations are implemented by distinct methods, each labeled with the method selector.

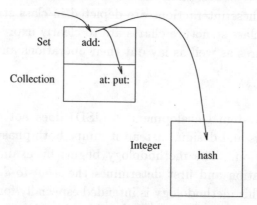

Figure 2.10: Representing classes and methods

The diagrams as explained above are quite suitable for small programs. However, classes are listed with the most specialized class at the top leading some designers to complain that it is not intuitive to place subclasses above superclasses. Another limitation implicates in the restrictiveness of the graphical elements in the diagrams, which are fitted to model Smalltalk programs, and likely to be employed during the implementation phase only.

As far as C++ is concerned, Ackroyd and Daum [72] suggest a basic graphical notation for classes, objects, functions and inheritance, as illustrated in Figure 2.11. The graphical notation adds numerous conventions for polymorphism, overloading, delegation, static variables and many other properties, enhancing graphical representation of object-oriented programs. Nevertheless, the notation is tied closely to C++ peculiarities, particularly those for private, protected and public members. Moreover, it is neither apparent how to use this notation for other programming languages nor how to employ it as a language-independent graphical notation for object-oriented design. Besides, the diagrams may depict extensive implementation details making them hard to apply to large and complex programs.

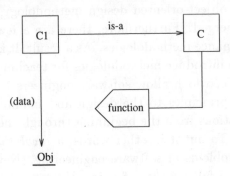

Figure 2.11: Notation for classes, objects, functions and inheritance

2.3. Results of the Classification

This chapter has briefly reviewed a number of object-oriented methodologies and outlined their power and oversights. There are dissatisfactions with current methodologies, which seem to place too much emphasis on designing for the task in hand and not enough on designing components for reuse nor designing with reusable components. From this survey, it is evident that further research on object-oriented methodologies is required in order to overcome the deficiencies and limitations of existing software development methodologies.

Most of the early methodologies that have appeared in the object-oriented arena, either induce to an implementation in Ada, which does not support inheritance, or disregard abstraction in terms of classes, and instead focus on object modelling. Other methodologies with the intention of combining existing structured methods together with object-orientation have led to the misuse of objects merely as data without regarding the operations on that data; the operations are treated separately as functions. Another setback with such combinations is the mapping of concepts from one approach to another. The adoption of different philosophies, the change of vocabulary and notation can confuse designers about which one should be used in which phase of the software life cycle.

Therefore, it can be concluded that so far there has been no generally accepted object-oriented design methodology, just limited attempts have emerged. Furthermore, there are a few, if any, object-oriented maintenance methodologies. As a result, it is the intention of this textbook to introduce methodologies for teaching software design and maintenance, which allow software engineers to apply powerful object-oriented principles to the design and maintenance of a wide range of applications from the beginning through the end of the software life cycle. To put it in other words, a *revolution* is still needed to tackle the problems of software engineering. New methodologies which exploit the full benefits of object-thinking within a substitute software life cycle model have to be pursued.

The next chapter describes an approach that yields a single coherent object-oriented methodology, rather than separate methods to solve certain parts of a design. Such a methodology must pay attention to object-oriented concepts already discussed, such as, classes, objects and inheritance. The proper use of these concepts can lead to a truly general object-oriented design methodology as independent as possible of any programming language. Moreover, reusability should be emphasized as part of the methodology within an alternative software life cycle model. Another objective of this book is to propose a

CASE environment to design object-oriented software. The environment should offer diagram editors and checkers, and encourage the use of reusable components to build software. All these topics are covered next.

Exercises

1. How would a paradigm guide a designer to one type of solution, whereas another paradigm would encourage a different solution?

2. Compare and contrast the functional decomposition approach and an object-oriented approach to software development.

3. How can one ensure that changing from structured development to object-oriented development lead to positive improvement?

4. How can object-orientation be accommodated within existing software development practices?

5. Is object-thinking a natural way to build software?

6. Exemplify the difficulties (such as ambiguities, fuzziness and vagueness) in using natural language descriptions to derive a design from.

7. What about describing a design with a concise narrative description plus a consistent graphical notation?

8. If informal methods are not perfect, what about formal methods for software development?

9. In an object-oriented design, the components are functionally independent. Explain.

10. What features should a generic software development methodology have?

11. Draw a list of criteria for assessing an object-oriented design methodology.

12. How much "inspiration" and "transpiration" is required when using a design methodology?

13. Is it possible to draw a clear line between object-oriented analysis and object-oriented design?

14. "Using the same software development methodology for every kind of application is a bad idea". Comment.

15. "The development of large and complex object-oriented software requires a revolution, not merely better versions of currently used software development methodologies". Discuss.

CHAPTER 3

OBJECT-ORIENTED DESIGN

It has been claimed that software systems developed following object-orientation can be significantly more elegant than those constructed applying a traditional structured approach, and that more software components can be reused during their development. However, using an object-oriented programming language does not, by itself, guarantee miraculous results. Like any other engineering activity, methodologies play an important role during the design of object-oriented software.

Software design is a creative process and there exist no algorithms for successful design, therefore it cannot be completely formalized. Thus, it becomes impossible to present designers with a recipe that will always lead to favourable results. Design is still an art dependent on the skills, intuition, creativity, wisdom and experience of the designer.

It is also difficult to quantify the "goodness" of a design or deciding whether a design is better than another. Nevertheless, the most general definition of a satisfactory design is one that meets the system requirements and costs as little as possible. Moreover, the design should be readily understandable, that means, it should exclude low level implementation details; and be modifiable, that is, components should be as independent of other components as is practically possible. In addition, repeatability is an important principle for a design methodology, in that, if two designers face similar problems and follow similar principles, they have to create equivalent software solutions.

Former chapters have presented aspects related to the object-oriented paradigm and the advantages achieved when it is applied. A variety of existing methodologies have been examined and their strengths and weaknesses have been pointed out. As can be seen from previous chapters, although the general principles of abstract data types, modularization and encapsulation are generally accepted as advantageous mechanisms for software design, there is little agreement on a general design methodology or a notation for representing an object-oriented design. Indeed, so far there has been a proliferation of such notations rather than a single well-known and widely used.

This chapter introduces a Methodology for Object-Oriented Design called **MOOD** [73], which is based upon, and obtains the benefits of object-orientation as presented in Chapter 1. MOOD promotes software design following object-thinking and it is independent of the idiosyncrasies of any specific programming language. The chapter contains five sections. The first section places the methodology into the context of software development. In broad terms, MOOD starts with an abstract model of the application and ends with a design ready to be implemented. Between these two representations there are steps that guide the designer throughout software design.

The steps which must be followed in order to design a software system using MOOD are discussed in Section 2. Such steps help the designer identify classes, build class hierarchies using inheritance, pick out objects and understand the software behaviour, as well as express the design graphically with four types of diagrams. This section also reveals a means for partitioning a large system into manageable pieces; this partitioning is based on the functionality of the software.

Section 3 highlights some benefits and drawbacks of the described methodology. The fourth section presents the main requirements for a CASE (Computer-Aided Software Engineering) environment to back an object-oriented design methodology. This chapter concludes with final remarks on MOOD, outlining some of the issues that should be examined when designing object-oriented software. Additionally, the last section presents a summary of the methodology steps.

3.1. The Context of MOOD

The software designer should start the work with an abstract model of the application which is accomplished through a system analysis. This abstract model is the first representation of the software system. But what should the system analysis be? System analysis is the study of an application for the purpose of understanding its essential features. It is characterized by obtaining information about the application; hence this information is non-structured, often incomplete and sometimes contradictory. The system analysis process then produces a description in terms of the requirements and objectives of the software.

Methodologies which attempt to give support for system analysis should consider the possibility of dealing with an incomplete abstract model and describing partial aspects of the application, then refining and complementing that abstract model. The result of system analysis comes as a graphical or textual, informal or formal, abstract model of the application. The more complete and consistent it is, the better. Therefore, system analysis is a means to understand the application. The purpose of an abstract model is to provide a description (graphical or textual, informal or formal) of the application.

MOOD begins with the abstract model of the application as input and assists in the production of a `design model` as output. The design model comprises a `static model` and a `dynamic model`. The static model is a generic representation of the software employing a set of diagrams that displays a global view of the software classes and components, also known as `static design`. The dynamic model depicts the behaviour of the software system, also termed dynamic design. Figure 3.1 shows, within the dashed rectangle, the context of MOOD. Although the boundary between each representation is usually fuzzy, the abstract model of the application, the design model and the program are three different, yet related abstractions of the software.

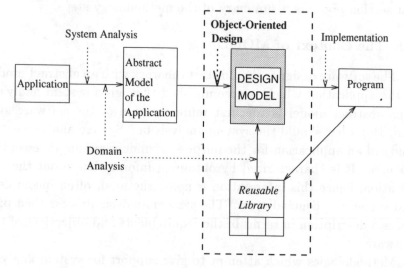

Figure 3.1: The context of MOOD

MOOD consists of a sequence of steps which helps designers refine an abstract model of the application. By using the methodology, designers could either start by identifying classes or considering object interactions. It has to be emphasized that the use of MOOD is aimed at keeping as close a connection as possible between the application and the object-oriented software by exclusively symbolizing real-world entities through classes, objects and inheritance.

It is often affirmed that the distinction between system analysis and design is that system analysis states "What" to build and design indicates "How" to build. Therefore, during the system analysis, the question "What is the software supposed to do?" should be answered. On the other hand, during the design the question "How should the software do what is stated during the system analysis?" has to be addressed. This distinction contains some important truths but ignores other subtle issues. For instance, is there any clear boundary between object-oriented system analysis and object-oriented design?

This is hard to answer because software development may be seen as a process of creation, manipulation and refinement of abstractions. When creating or transforming an abstraction, the designer actually deals with different representation of these abstractions. In order to make the refinement from one abstraction to another as simple and as free from error as possible, it must be easy to relate one abstract representation to the next. This requires abstractions to be related to one another, so that concepts introduced in one notation should be found in the other. Object-thinking allows designers to create abstractions which are close to the application (or to its abstract model), and to manipulate these abstractions throughout software development. It means that system analysis features can easily creep into design. Therefore, within an object-oriented framework, it is even more difficult to draw a distinct line between system analysis and design.

As far as the reusable library is concerned (see Figure 3.1), it contains a collection of reusable components, from both application and solution domains, put into and taken from there during software development. The use of a reusable library aims to select components which can be reused in the developing software. A reusable library requires an adequate scheme for classifying, storing and recovering components. The reuse of such components can take place in two manners: either directly when the component corresponds exactly to the one required, or through inheritance when there are slight differences, and specialization and generalization are necessary.

A software system is concerned with an application domain, and the clarification of the vocabulary for the application domain is one of the domain analysis functions. Domain analysis also plays a fundamental role in identifying potentially reusable components within an application domain. A comprehensive hierarchy of classes for an application domain supplies designers not only with reusable components, but also with potential parts for a software system. The essence of a sound object-oriented design is: design with reuse as well as design for reuse. That means finding application domain reusable components which can be taken from libraries as well as producing reusable solution that may be stored in a library.

A designer cannot be expected to have a perfect understanding of the system at the beginning of the design process. Rather, that understanding evolves through iterations and refinements with constant feedback, but each iteration makes the design model increasingly detailed. A top-down fashion for software development generally creates a system by successive refinements of software components. If the system is not trivially simple, it should be decomposed into large parts which may be further decomposed. Nevertheless, it is not easy for designers to divide a software system into components if the application is almost unknown. It could be argued that the top-down decomposition works better when a designer already knows the application domain. In contrast, following a bottom-up strategy would be more appropriate. These issues will be further discussed in the next chapter, but for now the MOOD steps are introduced.

3.2. Steps for Object-Oriented Design

In order to produce the design model following an object-oriented approach, it is necessary to identify and represent:

- software system classes;

- inheritance between classes;

- software behaviour in terms of object interactions.

An important aspect of MOOD is how the designer tackles the problem of designing in successive steps in order to produce the design model to be implemented subsequently. Briefly, the fundamental steps put forward by MOOD are:

- divide the system into manageable components;

- identify classes and/or objects which model the application;

- work out inheritance between classes;

- represent classes and inheritance;

- identify software behaviour in terms of objects and operations;

- represent software behaviour in terms of object interactions.

The MOOD strategy to tackling these steps is present in the next subsections. It is important to note that the sequence in which these steps are carried out depends on the knowledge that the designer has about the application domain, but this issue is examined in Chapter 4.

3.2.1. Representation of the Design Model

Graphical notations have been an integral part of most engineering techniques. In fact, there are very few software engineering activities which do not benefit from some sort of graphical notation. The use of graphical notations has proved to be an effective mechanism for expressing a design because a clean graphical notation can outline the architecture of a system clearer than a textually-based notation.

A systematic approach to software design can be offered by a set of guidelines supported by a graphical notation applied to represent a software system. An efficient graphical notation should be simple, accurate and a reflection of the paradigm employed to build the software. Thus, a graphical notation chosen for object-oriented design should directly promote this paradigm, by catering representation for classes, objects and inheritance.

An important aspect of MOOD is the graphical notation which allows a straightforward visual representation of the object-oriented design. The graphical notation to be presented later in this chapter comprises different types of generic diagrams that goes hand in hand with MOOD. The diagrams are independent of any programming language, provide a high level representation of a design and span a broad range of object-oriented concepts without making any assumptions about implementation. The guiding principle behind the proposal of these diagrams has been to keep them as simple as possible.

There are four main types of diagrams:

- `Composition Diagrams`: elucidate the composition and decomposition of a software system in terms of its components.

- `Class Hierarchy Diagrams`: are a simple but effective way to display classes, their attributes and operations, and inheritance relationships.

- `Object Diagrams`: indicate relationships among objects based on requests for operations between them.

- `Operation Diagrams`: portray how operations are combined to contribute to a particular functionality.

Each diagram proposed by MOOD and used during a design must have a unique identifier. It is recommended that the identification should give a clue to the type, the number and the name of each diagram. The identification for a composition diagram could start with "CO", class hierarchy diagrams with "CL", object diagrams with "OB" and operation diagrams with "OP"; followed by the number and name of the diagram.

These diagrams are the principal means for expressing a design with MOOD. They constitute a graphical representation of the design as a whole and can facilitate communication among designers. The diagrams are composed of simple symbols, and their automated support by a CASE environment is discussed in Section 4. The number of different basic symbols is small, the symbols are unambiguous and the visual impact of the arrangements of the basic symbols connotes the semantics of object-oriented concepts.

These diagrams are integrated with each other, and the information presented in a specific diagram must be consistent with the same piece of information displayed in another diagram. For instance, the operations used in a certain operation diagram must be defined in any class of another class hierarchy diagram. Such interrelationships between diagrams makes them a powerful collection of graphical notations capable of clarifying the whole design. The next subsections delineate how to create these types of diagrams which are the means by which a designer represents a software system at design level when MOOD is applied.

3.2.2. Identification of Components

The development of large software imposes some peculiarities on the design process. Often, the design of a software system of any significant size must be divided among different designers or several people grouped into small teams. A large system will probably require numerous components making it burdensome to comprehend. This complexity can be mastered by first identifying large software components based on the required software functionality.

When should identification of components be introduced? Large components are more likely to be disclosed during the early stages of a design and can be further divided into subcomponents. In a small system, where just a few services are offered, identification of components may not be necessary. However, a large and complex system, providing a wide range of services, requires decomposition to be applied from the beginning of the design. Nevertheless, finding a suitable division into components for an object-oriented software still seems to be subjective.

Composition Diagrams

Composition diagrams can be used to clarify all or parts of a software in terms of its components. Composition diagrams portray aggregations of components, where components are any software items such as subsystems, modules, classes or objects which make up the software. A component may also be subdivided into smaller subcomponents and vice versa, for instance, interdependent and cooperating components can be composed to offer a particular service.

Each component in a composition diagram fulfils the role of a software item in terms of the functionality supplied by that component. Figure 3.2 illustrates a composition diagram in which a CASE environment can be composed of three different components representing the tools (*graphic-editor*, *text-editor* and *checkers*) of the environment. This figure also shows how the *checkers* can be composed of its subcomponents (*consistency* and *completeness*). Each component is symbolized in the diagram by an ellipse. It is not the intention of composition diagrams to capture all the details of a system, rather its purpose is simply to represent broadly the components of the software. The relationship between large components and classes will be examined later in this section.

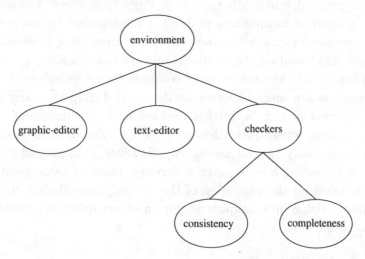

Figure 3.2: A composition diagram for a CASE environment

3.2.3. Identification of Classes

A class is the single most important concept for an object-oriented design. Identification of classes in MOOD involves the recognition of important classes in the abstract model of the application. Nevertheless, there is no easy and fast way of deciding what is and what is not a proper class. Part of the identification process is to assess the consequences of including or excluding potential classes. Defining abstractions in terms of some classes depends on the purpose they play in the software as a whole.

Finding classes requires several iterations before a suitable collection of candidate is determined. This is part of an iterative process for object-oriented development presented in Chapter 4. Iterations are not a sign of bad design and should be regarded as a healthy process by which learning takes place. The number of iterations depends on the level of knowledge that designers have about the application domain, as well as on their intuitions and skills gained through insight and experience. As a result, it is possible to give only guidelines that assist in determining the right classes for a certain design.

Firstly, the designer needs to understand the notion of class and what may be a class in the software system. Candidate classes can be:

- Abstractions of things: e.g. books, planes, sensors.

- Abstractions of people: e.g. professors, students, engineers.

- Abstractions of concepts: e.g. departments, graphics, flights.

- Roles played by things, people or concepts: e.g. people are *voters* for politicians or *taxpayers* for the government.

- Relationships between abstractions of things, people and concepts: e.g. people *purchase* things, people *marry* people.

As indicated in the first chapter, other important notions associated with classes are attributes and operations. As far as identification of attributes and operations is concerned, designers should study the abstract model of the application and take into account services supplied by a class, which can be initially identified as its operations. In order to delineate services, for each class the designer should answer these two questions:

- Which operations can be performed on instances of this class?

- Which actions do the attributes of this class undergo?

At the end of this stage, a set of classes which provide abstractions for conceptual entities of the real-world application, and their attributes and operations are identified. Thus, the design can be viewed as a collection of classes. A graphical notation to represent classes is discussed in the next subsection.

3.2.4. Identification of Inheritance

Identifying classes is simply the first step to design object-oriented software. After some classes have been selected, they can be related to one another to form class hierarchies. The notion of inheritance plays a key role during object-oriented design because it helps the designer derive new classes from primitive ones by exploiting their commonalities in terms of attributes and operations, so that class hierarchies are built.

Inheritance enables designers to create an extra class merely by specifying the differences between the new class and an existing one, instead of starting from scratch each time. As a design technique, the use of inheritance is similar to a stepwise refinement approach where inheritance arranges the classes which model an application into hierarchies of classes. Thus, inheritance is applied to create additional classes as specialization or generalization of existing ones.

Although formal or automated techniques for refining class hierarchies do not exist, there are a few rules that might assist in reorganizing a collection of classes into hierarchies. The main rule for building a class hierarchy is to figure out common attributes and operations and migrate them to a superclass, then eliminate from the superclass those operations that are frequently overridden in its subclasses rather than inherited by these subclasses. This rule makes the superclass more abstract and hence more generally usable (and reusable!).

In order to introduce inheritance, designers must settle upon a collection of primitive classes from which all others can be derived, by using the generalization and specialization mechanisms. A common example of inheritance by generalization can be noticed when a *basic-screen-window* class is created as a superclass from the *coloured-window* and *framed-window* subclasses. Such a superclass embodies the minimal characteristic of all screen windows. The two subclasses could add other properties to the *basic-screen-window* class by including such attributes as *foreground-colour* plus *background-colour*, and *border-width* into the subclasses respectively.

As far as inheritance by specialization is concerned, designers should try to clear up classes that cannot properly describe all their instances. In this case, two or more specialized subclasses can be derived. It is possible to specialize within a subclass the general properties defined in its superclass. A trivial illustration of inheritance by specialization is the following one: consider a *vehicle* class, with attributes *licence-number*, *maker* and *model*. This class can be further specialized into *freighter*, *bus* and *car* subclasses. This hierarchy of classes can be depicted textually employing the indentation scheme below:

- *vehicle* class: *licence-number*, *maker* and *model* attributes;

  - *freighter* subclass: *licence-number*, *maker*, *model* and *permitted-load* attributes;

  - *bus* subclass: *licence-number*, *maker*, *model* and *number-of-passengers* attributes;

  - *car* subclass: *licence-number*, *maker*, *model* and *nationality* attributes.

The *freighter* subclass could be further specialized into *van* and *lorry* subclasses. The attributes of the *vehicle* class are inherited by its subclasses, for example, a *lorry* object has the *licence-number* attribute from the *vehicle* class, as well as the *permitted-load* attribute from the *freighter* class, besides its own attributes (e.g. *number-of-axles*). A *lorry* object could now be handled either as a *vehicle* object, as a *freighter* object, or as a *lorry* object itself. The different viewpoints imply restricted visibility of the attributes, and make it possible to handle all subclasses simply as a *vehicle* class, whenever that is desirable. Attributes and operations of the superclass are available to their subclasses and new attributes and operations can be specified within the subclasses.

Having identified the primitives classes that may form the basis for the software system, the designer can also make use of the set theory in such a way that intersections between sets of attributes and operations of different classes can be singled out and inheritance naturally becomes visible. Venn diagrams are a convenient means of explaining sets and can be put to use as a technique to assist in the application of inheritance as well. A Venn diagram can give a hint of potential superclasses by showing which attributes and operations are held in common among classes. If two or more classes share some attributes or operations, they could inherit them from superclasses. If a common superclass does not already exist, the designer should create one and move the shared attributes and operations to it.

A procedure for identification of inheritance from Venn diagrams can be explained as follows: for each class define a set comprising the attributes and operations associated with that class and look for intersection between sets. The intersection may characterize a new superclass. The class hierarchy is created by pulling up the commonalities and by pushing down the differences. The main goal of this procedure is to place common attributes and operations as high as possible in the class hierarchy, so that more subclasses can share them. Figure 3.3 demonstrates two examples of identification of inheritance from Venn diagrams. In that figure, the letters 'A', 'O' and 'C' symbolize attributes, operations and classes respectively.

The following kinds of changes to the collection of classes are to be expected during the evolution of a design while class hierarchies are being created:

- add new classes to the collection;

- modify the attributes and operations of a class;

- reorganize the class hierarchy applying the specialization and generalization mechanisms.

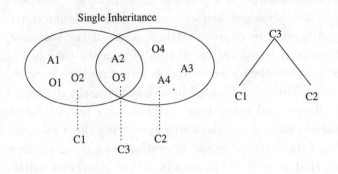

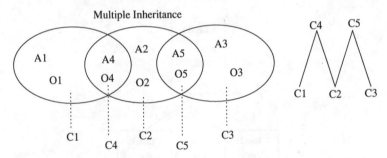

Figure 3.3: Identification of inheritance from Venn diagrams

Designers may modify a class either to add or delete some attributes or operations. They can also define additional classes if new key abstractions are discovered. The reorganization of the class hierarchies takes the form of changing inheritance relationships, adding new generic classes and shifting attributes and operations in the class hierarchies. This happens frequently at the beginning of the design and then stabilizes over time as designers better understand the key abstractions.

Class Hierarchy Diagrams

Class hierarchy diagrams in MOOD show the existence of classes and their relationships in a software design. Such diagrams depict how classes are arranged hierarchically. The designer can use class hierarchy diagrams to express static aspects of the software, by adhering exclusively to a fixed set of symbols, as sketched in Figure 3.4. A rectangle symbolizes a class and is annotated with its mnemonic name. A class name is indicated in a class hierarchy diagram followed by its attributes and operations. A class may restrict its attributes and operations from other classes by specifying them as *public* or *protected*. Any other attributes and operations in a class will be regarded as *private*, that is, part of the details of that class, and neither visible to other classes nor inherited by its subclasses.

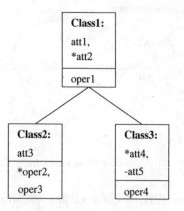

Figure 3.4: A generic class hierarchy diagram

A rectangle representing a class displays the externally visible (*public*) attributes and operations that instances of the class will possess. Subclasses derived from a superclass can, through the application of inheritance, make direct use of the *public* attributes and operations of the superclass. As well as *public* attributes and operations, the designer may wish to export additional attributes and operations which can be used exclusively by subclasses. These attributes and operations of a class are labeled *protected*, and will not be part of the normal interface of an object of that class. In the class hierarchy diagrams, *protected* attributes and operations are preceded by an asterisk ('*'), whereas *private* ones are anteceded by a hyphen ('–').

Relationships Between Class Hierarchies and Components

It is possible to divide a system following object-orientation by partitioning it into independent components and making a correspondence between the services covered by each component and the operations of different classes in the class hierarchies. Large components offer functionality at a high level of abstraction, to be fulfilled by operations of various classes, and a class is associated with a component only if it contributes to the service offered by that component.

A large component may comprise a collection of logically related classes, each supplying different operations which, when put together, contribute to the utility required for the software. A certain component has nothing to do with a specific class hierarchy, but with the software functionality. Large components may utilize the services of several classes placed in different class hierarchies to contribute to the overall activities. In fact, it demonstrates that composition diagrams are orthogonal to class hierarchy diagrams.

The correspondence between a large component and classes characterizes a `context` where functionalities are provided by a set of operations of different classes, as drawn within dashed lines in Figure 3.5. In this figure, the dotted lines reveal links between objects of different classes. A context consists typically of a set of classes, connected either by inheritance relationships or by a well-defined pattern of interaction between the objects of these classes via operations. A context groups classes together, so that a portion of the overall system functionality can be covered. The contexts maintain traceability between classes and functionalities; indirectly, a context depicts the classes related to a particular component.

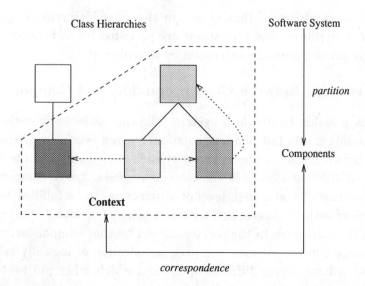

Figure 3.5: Correspondence between components and classes

3.2.5. Identification of Objects

This step is concerned with objects and concentrates on when and how they are created, destroyed, accessed and changed. An object in the sense of an object-oriented design is a set of operations gathered together with attributes, instantiated from a class. Some characteristics of object-oriented design regarding objects are:

- Objects are instances of some class.

- Objects can be created and destroyed.

- Operations are related to objects.

- Attributes are encapsulated into objects, so that other objects may have access only via operations.

- Requests are sent between objects to invoke operations or return results.

- Functionalities can be provided by operations from several objects.

Concrete entities in an application domain, such as people and things, are very likely to be objects in the software system. Therefore, they should be the initial targets to be picked out as objects. Identification of objects involves:

1. Understanding the application.

2. Depicting its main entities as objects.

3. Identifying the attributes of the objects.

4. Working out the operations on the objects.

5. Focusing on interaction between the objects.

Identification of objects is also important because it helps understand the dynamic behaviour of the software in terms of object interactions. The control flow of the operations defining the sequence in which the operations are requested can be figure out as well. The representation of software behaviour consists mainly of a network of objects manipulated by operations. Each object has its own internal states and is linked to the network through requests which establish the order of the operations. To understand the interaction among objects, it is necessary to identify:

• operations requested by an object;

• operations offered by an object;

• relationships between the objects;

• exceptional conditions within the operations;

• operations that can change the state of an object.

All objects go through various states during their lifetime, which means that they assume different states, defined by the values of their attributes. An object is in exactly one state at a time and its current state is recorded in its attributes. Only an operation associated with an object can change the state of the object.

The states that an object assumes can be displayed in a `state transition diagram`. Such a diagram shows the states of an object and the events which cause a transition from one state to another. A state transition diagram can represent the behaviour of an object over a period of time through the states which an object passes and the events which cause that change of state. Designers should look at the objects, viewing them as state machines and set the events applicable to each state. State transition diagrams can be used as a technique to assist them in understanding the operations on objects because the events that provoke the change of state of an object can be regarded as operations on the object. Each event may have conditions associated with it, and these conditions must be satisfied in order to have an operation triggered.

Figure 3.6 outlines a state transition diagram for a *screen-window* object. In this figure, the labels in bold express the various states which a *screen-window* object can go through. The labeled arrows convey events and possible operations on the *screen-window* object, as well as the effects these events have on the state of that object. Some operations cause a change of state when the object is in a certain state only, for instance, the *edit* operation has no meaning if the *screen-window* object is closed. These constraints are helpful to understand the behaviour of the application.

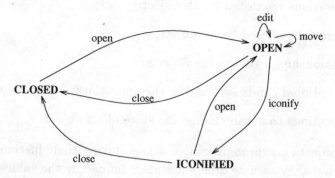

Figure 3.6: State transition diagram for a *screen-window* object

Object Diagrams

The graphical notation to be introduced in this subsection helps capture the software behaviour by employing object diagrams. Such diagrams outline objects and the requests for operations on other objects. A request connects one object to another when one object demands another to execute an operation. A request also depicts the dependency between a client object (the one that requests an operation) and a server object (the one that performs the operation). An object diagram is simply a network in which the nodes symbolize objects, and arcs connecting them represent operations. The interactions between objects happen one at a time; concurrency and parallelism are not considered in such diagrams.

Figure 3.7 displays an object diagram. An object is represented by a circle containing its identification and the class from which the object has been instantiated. Each object has a unique identifier that allows it to be referenced unambiguously within its class. A line entering an object denotes an offered operation and a line leaving an object represents a requested operation. Object diagrams partially elucidate the overall pattern of communication in the software system as they show which objects request which operations from other objects.

The object diagram illustrated in Figure 3.7 portrays the behaviour of some objects while a hypothetical tool is invoked within a CASE environment. When an *atool* object (from the *tool* class) manipulates an *awindow* object, the *awindow* object in turn can display a warning message *awarn* object and gets its state updated in a window manager *amanager* object. When an *atool* object is called, it can open an *awindow* object that may also be moved, edited, closed and iconified. An *awindow* object can also set a warning message *awarn* object to appear on the screen and this warning disappears after an *ok* operation occurs. A window manager *amanager* object can receive a request to update the position of an *awindow* object. It can also be noticed that a client object (an *atool* object) controls the requests to its server object (an *awindow* object).

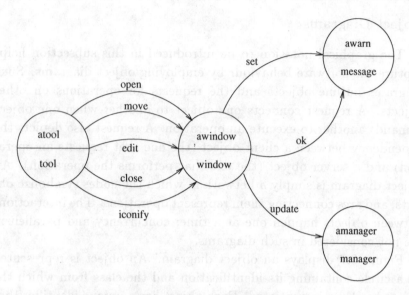

Figure 3.7: An object diagram for objects in an environment

3.2.6. Identification of Software Behaviour

Object-oriented software can be regarded as having a group of objects together with a design that establishes a detailed order of interaction on and between objects. These interactions characterize the behaviour of the software system. It is essential to clarify the dynamic behaviour of a system in terms of the control flow which defines the pattern of interaction between objects. Therefore, software behaviour focuses on when objects are created, accessed, changed and destroyed, as well as how objects interact with each other.

The required functionality is fulfilled as patterns of interactions between objects. The designer should consider the sequence in which the operations must be performed. In order to understand the software behaviour, four points are important:

- Which operations are performed.

- Which attributes are manipulated.

- When the operations are performed.

- How the operations are executed.

Answering the following queries is a useful way to determine the behaviour of a software system:

- Which objects do adequately provide specific functionalities?

- When are objects created and destroyed?

- When are objects accessed and changed?

- Which requests are needed in order to offer a required service?

- Which activities do the objects participate in?

- Which functionalities do the objects contribute to?

- When does an interaction between two objects take place?

As design details are expanded, it is natural to realize that in order to define the software behaviour and offer a certain service, several operations can be involved, which means that one operation of one class should call other operations on objects of other classes and may get some results. The pattern of these invocations establishes the `control flow` of the system and delineates how a specific service can be accomplished. There are basically two different trends which can be used to express the control flow of an object-oriented system, namely centralized and decentralized control flow:

- For a `centralized control flow`, there is always a client object that acts as a scheduler. When a server object finishes executing an operation, the control returns to the client object before the next operation is requested.

- For a `decentralized control flow`, there is not a distinct object that gives an overall view of the activities inside the system, but the control flow is spread out among several objects. To invoke an operation, a request is sent to an object. Such an object can send other requests to other objects and the control flow passes between objects until the execution of the software is over.

At the end of this step, software behaviour is modelled in terms of interactions between objects. The understanding of the behaviour is completed when the main objects in the system have been identified and the pattern of interaction upon these objects has been elucidated. Operation diagrams, as sketched below, depict the behaviour of a software system.

Operation Diagrams

The utility of a software is indicated by the services offered by its classes, and can be supported by one single operation or a combination of operations. Nevertheless, a class alone usually cannot supply enough operations to meet the demands of complex activities. Therefore, a set of operations need to be arranged together, so that a special service can be offered. For instance, to provide the "landing" functionality for an object of an *airplane* class, it is necessary to request operations to manipulate the ailerons in its right and left wings. These wings might be objects of two *leftwing* and *rightwing* subclasses of a *wing* superclass, in which the operations to control the movements of the ailerons are defined. Hence, the "landing" functionality is accomplished by requesting operations of two other distinct classes (*leftwing* and *rightwing* classes).

An operation diagram is a graphical representation conveying how operations can be combined. Operation diagrams are important because they clarify:

- which, when and where operations are used;

- relationships between operations of different classes;

- which operations contribute to a particular functionality.

An example of an operation diagram is drawn in Figure 3.8. A rectangle symbolizes an operation and is annotated with the operation name together with the class name where the operation is specified. This figure displays an operation diagram to draw a polygon on a screen window together with its possibly connected label; the polygon is then stored in a database.

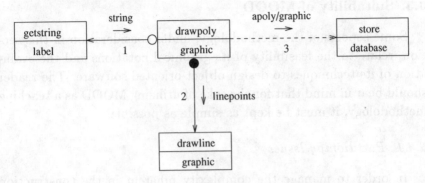

Figure 3.8: Operation diagram for drawing a polygon

In an operation diagram, a solid arrow means that a caller operation requests a called operation and gets the control flow back after the invoked operation is completed. A dashed arrow is used when a caller operation requests a called operation which either retains the control flow or passes it to yet another operation. An open circle at the beginning of an arrow denotes a conditional transfer of control flow, whereas a filled circle indicates an iteration. The numbers dictate the order in which the operations are requested.

As operation diagrams focus on the system control flow, they also have to show information and results which might be passed between operations. Each operation has a signature that determines the parameters involved in the requesting of the operation. Parameters are split into input and output parameters. Input parameters are provided by the caller operation and can only be accessed by the invoked operation, they are never changed. On the other hand, output parameters can be updated only by the called operation and are available to the caller operation. Parameters are designated by small arrows beside the operation they are related to (see Figure 3.8). Objects can also be parameters and in such cases the class to which the object belongs must appear to the right after the name of the object, separated by a slash. Thus, operation diagrams also enable designers to trace the information flow.

3.3. Suitability of MOOD

Some aspects of the methodology, under consideration in this section, relate to the feasibility of its graphical notations and the evaluation of its techniques to design object-oriented software. The reader should bear in mind that for the sake of utilizing MOOD as a teaching methodology, it must be kept as simple as possible.

3.3.1. Partitioning Issues

In order to manage the complexity inherent in the construction of large software systems, the decomposition of such systems into a number of smaller parts, which can be seen as large components, is advisable. The main purpose of such partitioning is to correlate some classes to a context that provides a specific functionality. Hence, the division should be based on the services offered by various components.

This observation leads to the following conclusions about the relationship between functionalities and classes. The notion of class hierarchy is not enough to divide object-oriented software into manageable pieces. It is important to realize how orthogonal the concepts of inheritance (employed in class hierarchies) and composition (associated with functionality) are. Inheritance can be taken to express an is-a relationship (i.e. an integer is a kind of number), whereas composition expresses a has-a relationship (i.e. a number has digits). Therefore, while class hierarchy diagrams aim to express generalization and specialization classes, composition diagrams convey aggregation and decomposition of components. As a consequence, composition diagrams had to be introduced to MOOD in order to supplement class hierarchy diagrams. Together, such diagrams enable the methodology to adequately represent large software systems.

3.3.2. Inheritance within MOOD

A few comments on the application of inheritance can be made at this point. There is a possibility that inheritance can be misused to aggregate attributes. It is a frequent mistake to consider a superclass and then try to derive subclasses from the meaning of the attributes making up the superclass. To illustrate, take a *car* class as the main class in a software system. A car could be divided into engine, transmission, brakes, suspension and so on. An engine can be further split into components such as ignition, fuel-injection, starter and so forth. Nevertheless, an *engine* class must not be viewed as a subclass of a *car* class because an engine is just a part of a car and it is not a specialization of a car. Certainly, the attributes and operations applied to a *car* class are totally different from those applied to an *engine* class.

The two most important concepts connected to inheritance should be specialization and generalization, never composition. The philosophy behind the correct use of inheritance should be: apply inheritance as a specialization or generalization mechanism only. Successful use of inheritance depends on employing a methodology that enforces or guides the application of these mechanisms. The utilization of Venn diagrams as recommended by MOOD helps prevent such misuse of inheritance because the intersections between the set of attributes and operations of the above *car* and *engine* classes would be empty, thus, the former should not be a superclass of the latter.

Despite class hierarchies being a crucial aspect of object-orientation, some setbacks associated with a large number of classes and multiple inheritance should be noticed. Experience has shown that large class hierarchies overwhelm designers when they attempt to understand the overriding process, especially when many levels of subclasses are used and multiple inheritance occurs. Designers of deeply-nested class hierarchies have difficulties grasping the many different superclasses and subclasses, and their inherited properties.

Another common pitfall is to overuse inheritance. In this case a class hierarchy comprises too many subclasses, with not enough difference in functionality between such classes, leading to a fine granularity. That is, many classes with few attributes and operations. Although high granularity may offer better prospects for reuse, it makes the class hierarchies arduous to understand. Classes supplying the same sort of services should be merged. Two courses of actions are open: either merge similar classes into a new class, or make them subclasses of a common superclass providing the shared functionality.

Inheritance perhaps works best in the development of small systems, which are expected to require a small number of people to be constructed. Where there are many designers updating and extending the class hierarchies, it is very likely that communication problems will cause unawareness of a particular change in the class hierarchies made by a certain designer. The following recommendations can be proposed to avoid such mismanagement of class hierarchies:

- All classes must be indicated in class hierarchy diagrams.

- An experienced software engineer must manage large amount of class hierarchies.

- Software configuration management techniques should be applied to control versions of classes and to keep track of the history of a design.

- Browsers should permit a global view of the system architecture, so that designers can figure out their position in the software.

3.3.3. Representation of Control Flow

The decomposition of an object-oriented system disperses the control flow and obscures the operations defined in class hierarchy diagrams. Such dispersion is due to the spreading of the control flow among several objects, making the global control flow less visible in object-oriented software than in systems constructed under functional decomposition. A possible reason for such control flow divergence is that unlike functionally decomposed software, where a high level function is an abstraction of lower level subfunctions, object-oriented software can be seen as a collection of independent objects that may be virtually running in parallel.

This dispersion of control flow also brings about complications in treating `exceptions` because the exception handling mechanism is required to deal with exceptional conditions in many different circumstances. Trials should be extended to further investigate the effects of exception handling mechanisms upon the overall control flow when exception handlers are either put into superclasses and then inherited by their subclasses or placed into a special class hierarchy of exceptions.

3.3.4. Object Interactions

Requests are sequential in `synchronous communication`. A client object requests an operation and waits idly for a response from a server object before continuing execution, implying that a single thread of control is passed from one object to another. Such object interactions are simplistic and not rich enough to display all kinds of possible interactions between objects.

In `asynchronous communication`, a client object is free to take further action after requesting a specific operation from a server object. A client object may proceed concurrently without waiting for the server object to reply. Concurrency fits quite well within an object-oriented framework as the autonomy of objects makes them a natural unit for concurrent execution.

State transition diagrams are helpful to capture aspects of software behaviour and to reveal operations to be implemented by different objects. However, this technique has inherent limitations: in particular, the inability to express recursive applications, and the difficulties in detailing algorithms distributed between two or more different kinds of objects. On top of that, in many realistic real-world applications, there are simply too many events to be represented within a state transition diagram.

Software behaviour depends on the overall interactions among objects as well as on the control flow within each operation. Object diagrams and operation diagrams help comprehend the control flow within the software and make it possible to realize interaction patterns to achieve a specific functionality. Such diagrams have demonstrated themselves to be a useful design aid to understand the interactions between objects, and have proven a valuable means of clarifying the control flow of the vast majority of object-oriented software.

This section has provided some remarks on the experience acquired from designing and experimenting with MOOD. It can be summarized from such experience that the methodology brings in a few characteristics which could be considered inexpedient by someone, but it is believed that the benefits gained from the use of MOOD outweigh its drawbacks.

3.4. A CASE Environment for MOOD

The high cost and complexity of software development and maintenance, and the growing need for reusable software components, are some of the factors stimulating research into better methodologies and CASE [74] (Computer-Aided Software Engineering) environments. Undoubtedly, the aim of a methodology is to improve some (or all!) of the quality, reliability, feasibility, cost-effectiveness, maintainability, management and engineering of software. But actually putting a methodology into practice is almost impossible without a set of automated tools which backs the methodology. Thus, one requirement for CASE tools is that they promote a software development methodology by sustaining and enforcing the steps, rules, principles and guidelines dictated by that methodology.

A CASE environment can provide computer-aided support for a methodology through a set of tools which form that environment, and can bring many improvements in software quality and efficiency for software production. Without such supporting tools (or strong management pressure) there is no easy means of enforcing the use of the ideas behind a certain methodology. Software designers may then merely pay lip-service to the adoption of the methodology, at best resulting in a minimal improvement in productivity, at worst putting the whole software development in jeopardy. Hence, CASE tools are a vital requirement for any design methodology for these, and several other important reasons, as will be seen next.

The process of software design has many facets and stages, spanning high level design early in the process down to low level design, which is closely related to the implementation step of actually writing code. At different stages, the designer is likely to be manipulating different kinds of information – in an object-oriented methodology, a high level design might concentrate on aspects of the classes whereas lower level design would need to examine interactions between objects which are instances of those classes.

It is widely recognized that graphical notations have clear advantages over textually-based notations. Therefore it seems paramount that a set of graphical notations is employed to represent the different concepts within a methodology, with visually different notations being used to denote conceptually different ideas. This consequently suggests that the requirement for a CASE environment is for a set of tools to support the design notations, each tool specialized to cope with one particular notation, thus presenting just one aspect of a design. For example, one tool would depict the class hierarchy while another tool would display a picture of object interactions.

Even though a set of tools is required, it is clear that the information manipulated by them has to be interrelated. A set of tools isolated from each other will not be conducive to supporting the design process. Thus, it is fundamental that the tools are integrated in order to enable designers not only share information among tools but also smoothly switch from one tool to another as the needs arise.

Design is normally an iterative process. Hence, the ability to easily navigate among various tools and notations is valuable, so that designers are able to view concomitant facets of a design. Further, such capability is also vital for software reusability, which is something that a CASE environment must certainly promote. A designer must be able to browse through already-captured parts of previous designs in order to look for reusable components. Clearly, what is needed are techniques able to create, classify and relate components, followed by CASE tools to store, select and retrieve potentially reusable components, as will be detailed in the next chapter.

The CASE environment should also come with automated tools for consistency and completeness checking to ensure that the principles of the underlying methodology are being properly obeyed and that mistakes made by designers are pointed out. More often than not, several iterations take place during the design phase – indeed, the ability to build up a design from an outlined framework into which supplementary details are gradually filled in, after other issues have been considered, is a useful requirement.

The power of abstraction, which is at the heart of the design process, is to be able to ignore details until absolutely necessary. Therefore it is more appropriate for completeness and consistency tools to be separate from the other tools, permitting designers to manipulate incomplete notations without continual warnings from automatic checks provided by such tools. Checks can then be explicitly applied by the designers at appropriate points in the design process, for instance, when they feel that some part of a design is complete.

The user-interface to the tool set is perhaps the most important factor in producing a CASE environment that is acceptable, especially when graphical notations are being manipulated. Clearly, the tools need to be user-friendly, driven intuitively by mouse, icons and menus rather than being driven by a complex text-based command structure. It is not the purpose of this section to explore what being "user-friendly" involves. Here, it is merely assumed that a multi-window, mouse-driven computing environment is a prerequisite, as is offered by current workstations with bit-mapped screens.

Even with user-friendly interfaces, a common interface should be prevalent for all tools in the environment. An environment with n tools with m different friendly interfaces is not practicable. Tools which have similar behaviour, such as the tools manipulating different graphical notations for the methodology, must adopt a common interface and present a consistent view of the information independent of which tool is being used.

A CASE environment is often put to work in the production of sizeable systems as in general such systems are complex and require a large amount of interrelated information. In such circumstances, a CASE environment brings further benefits because it ideally:

- simplifies the traceability between different phases of the software life cycle;

- checks the rules that govern the syntax and semantics of the underlying methodology;

- enhances communication among people;

- offers a uniform means for software representation;

- encourages team work across several workstations;

- assists in keeping documentation updated through report generators;

- produces graphical notation from information stored in its database;

- manages coordination among software engineers in terms of assignment, deadlines and integration of tasks.

3.4.1. MOOD Tools

With the need to produce ever large and more complex systems, the use of design methodologies has become increasingly imperative. Of the many existing and proposed software design methodologies, it seems clear that object-oriented methodologies will be at the forefront of most future developments, and hold the promise of substantially enhancing the software development (and maintenance) process. Methodologies by themselves are not sufficient however, and to be really effective it is crucial that a methodology is supported by an integrated set of CASE tools promoting the ideas behind the methodology.

When a designer is faced with a modern methodology, the absence of any enforcement is likely to result in the continued use of traditional ideas (or misuse of new ideas) and hence the full benefits of the new methodology will not be reaped. The nature of the object-oriented paradigm by itself has been influencing the way CASE environments have been built because some tools are quite related to the paradigm, in that, they must manipulate large number of classes and objects as potentially reusable components. Therefore, some fundamental tools are necessary. Such as:

- **Library management tools** to allow the searching for potentially reusable components.

- **Browsers** to facilitate navigation through class hierarchies, storage and recovery of classes, and visualization of classes in terms of their interfaces, attributes and operations.

- **Object-oriented diagram editors** to support an object-oriented graphical notation in terms of classes, inheritance and object interaction.

Based on the diagrams presented earlier in this chapter and the requirements for a CASE environment discussed above, the following tools can be identified in order to build up a CASE environment that automates MOOD:

- A composition diagram editor.

- A class hierarchy diagram editor.

- An object diagram editor.

- An operation diagram editor.

Not only must these diagram editors assist in the drawing of MOOD diagrams but also ensure that the design being represented adheres to the rules and principles of the underlying methodology. Of course, at the end of a design, the classes and operations presented in object diagrams must be in accordance with those defined in class hierarchy diagrams. The MOOD tools should allow the consistency and completeness of a design to be tested, by checking the interrelationships of the design information in different diagrams, and pointing out any essential details which have been so far omitted from the design; for example, all objects, attributes and operation within a class must have unique names. Such tools simply complain about perceived problems but let the designer decides whether the complaints are valid or not and how to fix them.

A class browser knows about classes and class hierarchies and allows navigation while showing attributes and operations. Class hierarchies can become so complex that without a help of browsers it is laborious even to find the classes which are part of a design or components candidates for reuse. With browsers, the designer is able to examine the library of reusable components too. On top of that, inspectors permit the states of objects be accessed and even changed. These tools should handle the issue of feedback information, which is a vital part of a design, and provide documentation of a software system via a report generator that basically generates print-outs from the descriptions of the design model.

Finally, software configuration management is one of the biggest complications facing designers of large software. This activity is concerned with controlling the software evolution. During large software development with several people working together, they must be sure that having made use of a specific class, the version of that class will remain unchanged. It is also useful to keep track of different versions of classes which comprise a particular version of the software. All changes must be automatically logged, so that the re-creation of earlier versions and comparison between versions are feasible. Hence, a tool to perform the functions of software configuration management is vital. Therefore in the MOOD environment there must be other supplementary tools as well, such as:

- A consistency checker.

- A completeness checker.

- A class browser.

- A library management tool.

- An object inspector.

- A report generator.

- A configuration management tool.

These tools should give some freedom to designers, letting them make some temporary omissions and then checking for such mistakes later in the design process. Moreover, the tools must be integrated with each other through a uniform interface together with a common database used to store software system information (such as names of classes, attributes, operations and objects) making use of a single representation model, preferably an object-oriented model.

3.5. Observations on MOOD

Object-oriented software can be viewed from two different layers of abstraction, as portrayed in Figure 3.9. There is an upper generic layer that shows the static classes of the software, and a lower level layer which consists of objects and express software behaviour. The upper layer displays the set of classes from which any software may be constructed, while the lower layer reveals the actual objects and potential object interactions required in a particular software system. The design of each layer may be carried out simultaneously.

It is important to remember that identifying classes is not the same as identifying objects. Classes are a means of expressing static commonalities between objects and templates to create them, whereas objects will have a dynamic life in a running software. The MOOD diagrams represent both the static and dynamic aspects of a design. On one hand, the static design consists of class hierarchy and composition diagrams. On the other hand, the dynamic design is expanded

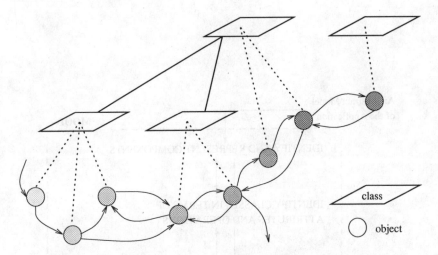

Figure 3.9: Static and dynamic layers of a software system

with both object and operation diagrams which indicate the overall dynamic behaviour of a system. At first, the operations on individual objects are presented in object diagrams and then these operations are combined to perform the functionality required from the software.

The steps put forward by MOOD, as discussed earlier in this chapter, are outlined in Figure 3.10. The steps emphasize design before implementation and are independent of any programming language. The design process begins with an abstract model of the application and culminates with a design model ready to be implemented. The path connecting these two models is not a straight line, but rather an iterative refinement process. In the course of building up an object-oriented software system, the steps involved in the design of necessary classes and objects are almost certain to be repeated many times.

Designers can apply MOOD to represent a software system by using exclusively a fixed set of diagrams. Composition diagrams to depict software components, whereas class hierarchy diagrams to show how classes are arranged hierarchically. Additionally, object diagrams and operation diagrams are used to clarify the software behaviour. The next chapter discusses reusability issues within the MOOD frame-

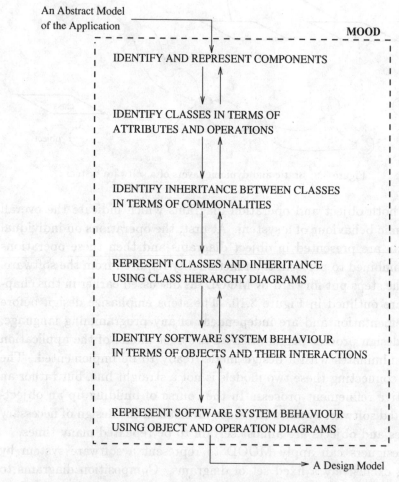

Figure 3.10: Steps recommended by MOOD

work and describes a software life cycle model which encompasses this methodology.

Exercises

1. What are your personal goals when designing a software system?

2. Which characteristics must be specified in an object-oriented software design?

3. Why is it difficult to measure the quality of a design?

4. Discuss the advantages of graphical notations and suggest applications where it would be more appropriate to use a graphical notation rather than a textual notation.

5. Use state transition diagrams to express changes in the states of:

   (a) A bulb.

   (b) A printer.

   (c) A floppy disk driver.

   (d) A car with automatic gear.

6. Take a real-world application of sending flowers to someone, and present a solution to this problem using of object and operation diagrams.

7. Use class hierarchy diagrams to create a static design of an electronic mail software.

8. Suggest components and classes for a library lending system.

9. Draft a design for the following applications:

   (a) Bank account management.

   (b) Airline reservation system.

   (c) Electricity power station control.

   (d) Manned space probe.

10. Define the terms completeness and consistency in a design. What is the best way to achieve these qualities?

11. Discuss the meaning of the term CASE. Outline the key features that a CASE environment should encompass.

12. Describe the benefits of using methodologies, manual or automated, in the design of software systems.

13. Which extra benefits are gained from the use of a methodology backed by a CASE environment?

14. Is a CASE environment much more than a collection of tools? In what sense tools are integrated in a CASE environment?

15. Why is it important that all tools in a CASE environment offer a uniform interface and a centralized database?

16. Organize the main components of a CASE environment making use of a onion-like diagram.

17. Suggest tools which should be included in a generic CASE environment to support the development of real-time systems, parallel processing systems, and process control systems.

18. Think of the disadvantages of CASE environments. What are the limitations of CASE tools?

19. "Most CASE environments are tied to a particular methodology and so involve a strong commitment to that methodology. This makes difficult to move ahead to new techniques". Discuss.

20. "A CASE environment does not make a bad designer good". Comment.

CHAPTER 4

REUSABILITY AND LIFE CYCLE ISSUES

This chapter discusses reusability and software life cycle issues which arise during the development and evolution of object-oriented software. The first section concentrates on existing mechanisms to achieve reusability, such as composition and inheritance. The section also outlines the main reasons why software is not extensively reused and examines the difficulties associated with reusability during the design phase. Additionally, in this section reusability is added to the foundation of the MOOD methodology.

In the second section, the main issues concerning an alternative software life cycle model are considered. The purpose of this section is twofold: firstly, to investigate how different levels of knowledge that a designer has about the application domain can affect software production; and secondly, to present a software life cycle which encompasses MOOD and takes reusability into account.

Section 3 covers other general aspects that form a more complete assessment of the whole software process. For instance, the most frequently used abstraction mechanisms, and an estimate of the time and effort spent on each phase of the described life cycle model. The chapter ends with comments on the object-oriented software process with regard to reusability, CASE tools and the software life cycle put forward.

4.1. Reusability During Object-Oriented Design

The concepts of reusability and object-orientation are so interrelated that it is often difficult to talk about one without mentioning the other [75]. This section describes an approach to software reuse while the design process is carried out. The strategy to be explained is in accordance with the design philosophy behind MOOD, in such way that while its steps are performed, reusability through composition, generalization and specialization mechanisms is considered.

The approach focuses on a collection of software systems within a certain application domain, and encourages reuse of software components from an existing reusable library for that application domain. It addresses the mechanisms employed when components are reused from the reusable library. Moreover, it recognizes the iterative nature of software creation, hence repetitions are incorporated into the reuse process where appropriate.

A diagrammatic representation of how reusability takes place within MOOD is portrayed in Figure 4.1. The reuse process is well-suited for object-oriented software development because the composition, generalization and specialization mechanisms, which are part of the object-oriented design process (as presented in Chapter 1), are considered. Underlying the reuse of software components, there are activities that address the identification of reusable components and their deployment into the developing system.

Reusability implies *design with reuse* and *design for reuse*. Initially, the software engineer identifies potentially reusable components from an existing reusable library, the components are then selected and reused through composition, generalization and specialization mechanisms. At the end of the software development, there may be many new potentially reusable components which need to be classified and stored into the reusable library. In the future, such components can be reused in other systems. The second issue will be examined later in this section.

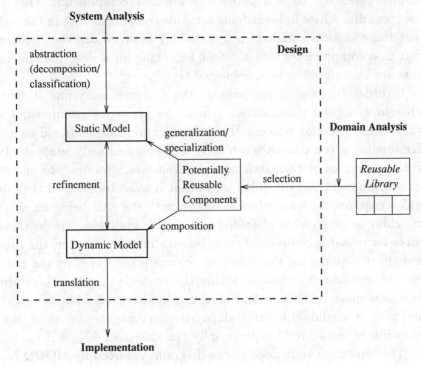

Figure 4.1: Reusability within MOOD

4.1.1. Relationships Between Components

So far, most of the work which has been done in the reusability arena involves storing and recovering components from reusable libraries, but there are yet many complications related to reusing such components. To illustrate, as software systems become mature, the libraries may grow as domain-specific reusable libraries and reusable components can be added over time. It does not take long for such libraries to expand to enormous proportions and often with multiple versions of a component, which makes it difficult for designers to look for components that might meet their needs.

Reusable libraries are usually large and their organization turn them problematic to find potentially reusable components. One of the great difficulties in identifying reusable components lies in the fact that there is a discordance in terminology between different people, that is, a component which someone is looking for is described in the libraries by unfamiliar or unexpected terminology.

In order to reuse a component, the designer must find it first. Therefore, a good classification scheme for arranging components is vital to the selection process. This classification can be an aid to understanding a component when software reuse demands adaptability of that component to match new requirements. Besides, the search for a component is a difficult task in that it must be selected the one which requires the least effort to adapt, with the goal being an exact matching between what is needed and what is available. The learning curve for reusable components may be substantial. However, the time and effort required for this selection process is decreased by the presence of semantic information within the reusable library. Therefore, designers must be able to find a connection between what is needed and what is available. Relationships between components can be used to facilitate the search for potentially reusable ones.

The semantics embedded in the diagrams enforced by MOOD can be expressed by relationships between components. For instance, has-a relationships are found in composition diagrams, is-a relationships are presented in class hierarchy diagrams, uses-a relationships are depicted in operation diagrams, and is-part-of-a relationships can connect a component to a particular context. Such relationships could be taken as a classification scheme to provide a network of predefined links between components, thus introducing some semantic information and a vocabulary into the reusable library.

A scheme for representing relationships between components of a reusable library entails on organizing them through a set of predefined relations. Such relations allow components to be classified and connected to others which can also be reused. In addition, relations express links between different components, facilitating the understanding of the components. Relations applied to express design information between two or more reusable components can help solve the problem of discordance of terminology between people because the relations establish fixed semantic information between components. Four different relations to link components and describe concepts associated with MOOD are proposed:

1. Compose (component-1, list-of-components): specifies component-1 as a combination of components in a list-of-components (has-a relationship). This information is available in composition diagrams.

2. Inherit (component-1, component-2): defines that component-1 is a generalization of component-2, or the other way round that component-2 is a specialization of component-1 (is-a relationship). This information can be found in class hierarchy diagrams.

3. Use (component-1, list-of-components): indicates that component-1 interacts with components in the list-of-components (uses-a relationship). It means that any operation of component-1 uses operations defined in any component in the list-of-components. A complete list of dependencies among operations of various components can be built with information from operation diagrams.

4. Context (component-1, context-1): associates component-1 with context-1 specified by the designer (is-part-of-a relationship). The context-1 can be a special application domain. This process requires classification of components and depends on the experience of the designer.

The compose, inherit and use relations can be perceived straight from the MOOD diagrams or, if necessary, complemented with other information provided afterwards, whereas the context relation should be made explicit by the designer. The relations presented may be viewed as an alternative textual notation to describe a software system.

Given that the information present in a reusable library is compatible with the information dealt with in the methodology, the MOOD diagrams as explained in Chapter 3 can be used to embody reusable components in the reusable library. Therefore, enquiries to a reusable library, which stores such relations and also manipulates the same concepts as MOOD, can be undertaken. Consequently, as the semantics of the diagrams can depict relationships between reusable components, reusability is naturally encouraged by the application of the methodology.

4.1.2. Reusability Process

The decisions involving the reuse of a component are very important in that, the one which requires the least effort to adapt must be selected, with an exact match between what is needed and what is available being the goal. Basically, the selection of a component from a reusable library imposes four steps:

1. Identify the required (*target*) component.

2. Select potentially reusable components.

3. Understand the components.

4. Adapt (specialize, generalize, compose or adjust) the components to satisfy the needs of the developing system.

The search for a component in a reusable library can lead to one of the following possible results:

- An identical match between the *target* and an available component is reached.

- Some fitting components are collected (partial match), then adaptations are necessary.

- The requirements are changed in order to fit available components.

- No reusable component can be found, then the *target* component must be created from scratch.

Following a procedure which helps select potentially reusable components is fundamental to the reuse process. The procedure detailed in Figure 4.2 illustrates a typical attempt to reuse a component from a reusable library. The procedure elucidates exclusively the selection of reusable components; classification and storage issues are considered later in this section. By properly classifying a component using the relations described previously, the chance of finding potentially reusable components is increased. Furthermore, the effort required to get a suitable component is reduced because the classification scheme based on relations can guide designers through the various components quickly and efficiently.

While searching for components it is necessary to address the equivalence between the *target* component and any near matching components. The best component selected for reuse may also require specialization, generalization or adjustment to the requirements of the new software system in which it will be reused. Sometimes, it is preferable to change the requirements in order to reuse the available components. The adaptability of components depends on the difference between the requirements and the features offered by existing components, as well as the skill and experience of the designer. The process of adapting components is the least likely to become automated in the reusability process.

4.1.3. Lifetime of Reusable Components

Reusability not only involves reusing existing components in a new software system but also designing components which are meant for reuse. While a software is being developed, it might be realized that some components can be generalized and reused in future software development. An important issue in the quest of reusability is how

```
begin
    //The process of component reuse
    given a key name (the name of the target component),
    search library for potentially reusable components and
        their relations

    if identical match between the target and an available component
    then
        //reuse by composition
        retrieve it and reuse it

    else
        collect fitting components

        for each collected component
            assess the degree of matching
        endfor
        rank and select the best component
        if the target can be a subclass of the best component
        then
            //reuse by specialization
            put the target as subclass and inherit commonalities

        else
            if the target shares commonalities with the best component
            then
                //reuse by generalization
                create a new abstract superclass,
                put the target and the best component as subclasses

            else
                //specialization and generalization are not convenient
                if possible
                then
                    adjust the best component to the requeriments or
                    adjust the requeriments to the best component

                else
                    //reusability is not possible
                    create the target component from scratch
                endif
            endif
        endif
    endif
end
```

Figure 4.2: A procedure to reuse a component

to make a potentially reusable component available to other people. The component must be understandable, well-written and well-documented. Finally, the component must be easily adaptable for different uses, either in original or in modified form. Therefore, developing reusable components is considerably more difficult and imposes much greater expense than producing ordinary components, although it may still be worth the investment.

Within the object-oriented paradigm, classes are the most important reusable components. Since an object-oriented software is developed essentially as an interrelated collection of independently developed classes, it is important to understand the stages that such components go through. The stages reflect the activities involving the identification, design, implementation, validation, classification, storage (with relations), refinement, selection and reuse of the component. Figure 4.3 clears up the lifetime of a reusable component.

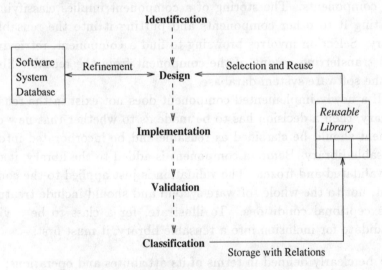

Figure 4.3: Lifetime of a reusable component

Through the promotion of the specialization, generalization and composition mechanisms during the design phase, application-dependent classes should be revised, so that they can be sufficiently generic to be of use in a wider range of applications rather than in the single system for which they were originally developed. This generality requires extra effort during the design and implementation phases in the short term, but in the long term, after a sufficiently broad reusable library is created, it will lead to a significant reduction in overall software development time and effort.

There must be in fact two main libraries: the reusable library from which components of interest can be picked up and to which new generic reusable components can be added, as well as the software system database that keeps information concerning a particular software under construction. Modification of components in the reusable library is not recommendable; a copy of the component should be taken into the software system database and refinements carried out there.

Tools can manipulate the reusable library by storing and selecting components. The storing of a component implies classifying it, relating it to other components and putting it into the reusable library. Selection involves browsing to find a component, retrieving it and transferring a copy of the component from the reusable library to the software system database.

If a newly implemented component does not exist in the reusable library, then a decision has to be made as to whether that new component should be classified as reusable and be incorporated into the reusable library. Before a component is added to the library, it must be validated and frozen. The validation is just applied to the component, not to the whole software system and should include treatment of exceptional conditions. To illustrate, for a class to be a viable candidate for inclusion into a reusable library, it must first:

- be clearly defined in terms of its attributes and operations;

- have a reasonable performance in terms of time and space required to execute its operations;

- be a generic abstraction, which means that the functionality it provides must be sufficient enough to model the real-world entities abstracted;

- have a robust behaviour if it is misused or pushed to its limits, that is, exceptions must be handled.

It is also very important to separate classes of client objects from server objects. Client objects are often application-dependent and they make decisions and switch the control flow among several server objects. Client objects should not directly perform calculations or implement complex algorithms. On the other hand, server objects perform specific and detailed operations, executing general computations to implement a certain self-contained algorithm and rarely change the control flow. Therefore, server objects are more likely to be reused in other systems than client objects since the former are more application-independent and basically wait to receive requests from client objects. Thus, as far as design for reuse is concerned, classes of server objects are preferable.

4.2. Object-Oriented Software Life Cycle Model

This section presents an alternative object-oriented software life cycle which encompasses MOOD. The life cycle model is influenced by the knowledge that the designer has about the application domain and also addresses reusability within an object-oriented approach to software production.

4.2.1. Role of the Knowledge about the Application Domain

People hardly ever solve a new problem from scratch. Instead, they try to figure out similarities between the new application and previously known applications and their solutions. By making suitable assumptions from acquired experience, people attempt to solve the new problem. This process is referred to as *solving by analogy*, and is considered to be a natural way by which people learn. The successful use of solving by analogy depends on recognizing similarities between problems and recalling solutions to analogous problems. Therefore, it can be assumed that the knowledge that software designers have about a certain application domain increases the chance of reusing solutions from that domain. Most of the current object-oriented methodologies do not take this human characteristic into account though.

When software engineers are developing software in an unfamiliar application domain they do not apply the same skills as when they are constructing software in a familiar domain. Of course, there are differences between the ways to produce software, depending on whether or not software engineers can use the knowledge obtained when they developed equivalent software in a well-known domain.

Experts explicitly create high level abstractions of a system, whereas novices think about low level entities and their behaviour within the system [76]. Therefore, the knowledge that software engineers have about an application domain affects the means by which software creation is carried out. Experts tend to rationalize in more abstract and high level terms following a top-down manner. On the other hand, novices usually start working with low level abstractions of the software and the development process is thus predominantly bottom-up.

A strictly top-down or bottom-up strategy to software production is not quite appropriate for the object-oriented paradigm. This section preaches a top-down or bottom-up style for software creation, taking into consideration the knowledge that the designer has about the application domain. This knowledge naturally determines the prevailing strategy to subsequent software development.

A designer who knows the application domain should start thinking about high level abstractions (such as class hierarchies), whereas another who does not know much about the application domain should begin instantiating some objects and trying to understand the low level software behaviour. As software construction proceeds, the designer may sometimes follow a mixed approach to software production, switching between a top-down and a bottom-up fashion as possibilities are explored. However, the predominant tactic is determined by the designer's knowledge about the application domain.

4.2.2. A Seamless Software Life Cycle

The creation of software is characterized by change and instability, and therefore any diagrammatic representation of a software life cycle model should consider overlapping and iteration between its phases. Based on the steps defined by MOOD, a consensus may be drawn on the phases pertinent to a *seamless* life cycle model and the common tasks performed following the methodology.

A software life cycle model which encompasses the methodology and takes reusability into account is indicated in Figure 4.4. Although the main phases may overlap each other and iteration is also possible, the planned phases are: system analysis, domain analysis, design (static and dynamic) and implementation. Maintenance is an important operational phase, in which bugs are corrected and extra requirements met; this will be thoroughly discussed in the next chapters.

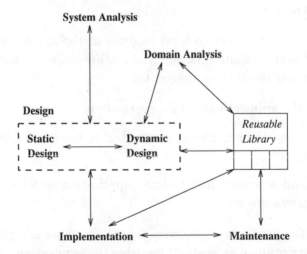

Figure 4.4: A seamless software life cycle model

An outcome of this software life cycle model is the emphasis on reusability during software creation and evolution, and the production of reusable components meant to be useful in future projects. This is naturally supported by the object-oriented paradigm due to inheritance and encapsulation. Reusability also implies the use of composition techniques during software development. This is achieved by initially selecting reusable components and aggregating them, or by refining the software to a point where it is possible to pick out components from the reusable library.

Figure 4.4 displays a diagrammatic representation of how the system analysis, domain analysis, design, implementation and maintenance phases proceed iteratively over time and how reuse of components from the reusable library is taken into consideration within the software life cycle model. Reusability within this life cycle is smoother and more effective than within the traditional waterfall model because MOOD integrates at its core (through `relations` associated with its diagrams) the concern for reuse and its mechanisms, as shown in the previous section.

System Analysis

This phase involves high level analysis of the application for the purpose of understanding its essential features. The system analysis phase demands the system analyst to:

- study the application and its constraints;

- understand the requirements expected to be satisfied by the software system;

- create an abstract model of the application in which these requirements are met.

One of the products of the system analysis phase is a graphical or textual description of an abstract model of the application. This phase may conduce to the identification of the major parts of the application, so that the system can be divided into large components based on the functionality that should be offered. A glimpse of the preliminary classes and objects which model the application can come up as well. If several similar objects are found, a class must be established. In the same way, if correlative classes have been identified, class hierarchies should be worked out.

At this stage, the services delivered by a software system helps figure out its subsystems and major components. However, as compared to functional decomposition, this phase is neither concerned with the details of functions in terms of algorithms, nor that functions can be refined into other subfunctions, but it worries over mapping the application in terms of components, classes and objects.

The result of this phase is an object-oriented abstract model of the application, which may be graphical or textual, using a formal or informal method, as the system analyst wishes. At this phase it seems unnecessary to detail classes in terms of their attributes and operations, or to look for communication patterns among objects of different classes, since what is more important is a high level view of the software.

Domain Analysis

Domain analysis involves the examination of a certain application domain and seeks to identify and classify entities which commonly occur in systems within the application domain in order to formulate concepts about that application domain. Thus, domain analysis is an activity which should be carried out at the beginning of software production.

The domain analysis phase primarily seeks to abstract and classify concepts which form the vocabulary of the application domain. At this stage a common terminology is drawn. Large applications should be broken into parts, so that specialists in a specific application domain can carry on the domain analysis in that application domain.

During this phase, the abstract model of the application comprising high level abstractions of software components may be refined and new classes and objects related to these components can be defined. Therefore, the boundary between system analysis and domain analysis may at times seems fuzzy because identifying key abstractions in the application domain may be viewed as part of system analysis or domain analysis. Nevertheless, at this level, domain analysis is also concerned with the identification and organization of potentially reusable components.

Selection of reusable components from former systems or from a reusable library must be considered. When performing domain analysis, the specialist might have a sketchy idea about candidate classes along with their attributes and operations. Subclasses can be derived from classes belonging to a special application domain, and objects can be instantiated from classes stored in a reusable library and then composed with other objects. Within this life cycle model, the main result of the domain analysis phase should be the reuse of software components already developed.

Design

Object-oriented design is an exploratory process. The designer looks for classes and objects trying out a variety of schemes in order to discover the most natural and reasonable way to model the application. There has been a tendency to present object-oriented design in such a manner that it looks easy to do. Nevertheless, in the design of large and complex software, identification of key classes and objects is likely to take some time. During the design phase the primary concern is to build a design model which fulfils the overall software functionality. The construction of the design model involves identifying relevant classes and objects, and producing both the `static design` and the `dynamic design`.

The static design comprises a static model of the system and basically makes use of class hierarchy and composition diagrams. The dynamic design consists of a dynamic model representing the software behaviour using object and operation diagrams. During the design phase those abstractions identified in previous phases are turned into representations expressing the software in more detail. The static design captures the generic and essential features of a system and can be expanded to other systems within the same application domain. In contrast, the dynamic design captures behavioural aspects of a certain system and is therefore more difficult to generalize to other systems.

When designers face an application, they should not ask "How do I work out a solution to this problem?". Instead, they should ask, "Where are the classes and objects that I can directly or indirectly reuse to solve this problem?". A procedure to guide them over this task is presented in Section 1. At this point, they should be able to examine a reusable library and to select components which closely match the classes and objects necessary to build the software.

A good browser is helpful to navigate the class hierarchies and trace the attributes and operations applicable to a specific object. One of the setbacks of object-oriented design is that in order to understand a class hierarchy it is often necessary to scan three or four super-classes to find out all attributes and operations that make up a class. Thus, a browser is of paramount importance to locate information in the class hierarchies. A browser can automatically connect all inherited attributes and operations to a sub-class together with the related super-class names. In this way, while the designer is browsing a class, all the properties of the class and of its super-classes are immediately available. Although browsers are very useful for discovering and understanding the characteristics of classes, they are by no means a sufficient tool for finding suitable candidate classes for reuse.

As more classes are identified along the design, re-evaluation of the complete set of classes is required. Repetitions are not unusual, since a good design usually takes several iterations. The number of reiterations also depends on the designer's insight, experience and knowledge about the application domain. A bottom-up strategy (instantiation of some objects) should be considered if the designer does not have a good perception of the application domain.

Some abstract classes picked out during the design phase should undergo further refinements (e.g. treatment of exceptional conditions) until they become generic and robust enough to be placed in a reusable library. This surely adds an overhead to software construction, which is more than compensated for by the long term savings when such components are reused in future projects.

Implementation

The implementation phase is characterized by the translation of a design model into an object-oriented programming language. The design model comprises static concepts and dynamic behaviour represented by the output of the design phase. In this phase the major tasks involve the implementation the identified classes, along with the cooperation among the objects, in order to fulfil the required software functionality.

The line between design and implementation is also a blurred one. Implementing a class requires defining the data structures reciprocal to attributes and the algorithms corresponding to operations of that class. It is also necessary to implement the control flow which realizes the interaction between objects and specify the overall software behaviour. The best idea is to isolate a class or an object and decide whether a component to match that class or object can be reused, or it has to be implemented from scratch.

Maintenance

During software maintenance, changes are introduced to a delivered software system. Such changes, as will be seen in the next chapters, are not meant only for correcting errors occurred in an operational software. These changes may be also for enhancing, updating the system to anticipate future errors or adapting the system in response to a modification in the environment. Thus, during the maintenance phase, software components may be accessed from, as well as new ones may be added to the reusable library of the concerned application domain. For instance, a change to adapt the software to a new environment may specialize already existing classes, so that characteristics of the new environment are taken into consideration, hence expanding the spectrum of environments the reusable components are able to deal with.

After changes are introduced to the system, an updated release of the software is generated. Therefore, maintenance of software system does not only allows the software to evolve but also the reusable library concerning the existing systems expands with the maintenance process of related software.

Table 4.1 summarizes the phases of the software life cycle model put forward in this chapter. This table shows the input, tasks performed and output of each phase, which evolves dynamically as the understanding the software engineer has about the system grows. The phases are traceable during software construction and evolution, as well as determine a *seamless* object-oriented software life cycle model.

Table 4.1: Input, tasks and output of each phase

Phases vs I/O	Input	Tasks	Output
System Analysis	application: user needs and software system requirements	create an abstract model of the application	abstract model of the application
Domain Analysis	abstract model of the application	identify possible reusable components	potentially reusable components
Design	abstract model of the application and potentially reusable components	build static and dynamic models (design model)	static (generic) and dynamic (behaviour) models
Implementation	static (generic) and dynamic (behaviour) models	implement the models	software system solution to the application
Maintenance	delivered software system plus changes to be introduced	implement the changes	updated release of the software system

4.3. Software Life Cycle Issues

This section contains some general issues related to the software life cycle model presented. The aspects to be discussed include the kinds of reusable components, the prevailing abstraction mechanisms employed in each phase of the life cycle model, and an estimate of the percentage of development time to be spent on each stage.

4.3.1. Types of Reusable Components

There are differences in the mechanisms used to achieve reusability when different kinds of reusable components are involved. The most basic software components (i.e. objects) are often reused by composition, which can be seen as a process of building a piece of software from elementary self-contained components. Nevertheless, from an object-oriented viewpoint, reusability is naturally accomplished by reusing classes through inheritance. In this case, it takes place by specialization and generalization of commonalities between classes. Not all classes identified early in the development process are implemented because some of them can be refined during the design phase or taken from a library of reusable components. It is better to reuse high level components such as classes during design because they have fewer implementation details which would limit their applicability.

There is a need for tools to support the creation of domain-specific collections of reusable components, also known as `framework`, which is tuned specially for a particular application domain, for instance, an interface-building framework. A framework could be viewed as a generic structure that provides a skeleton for designing software in a certain application domain. Building and tailoring software from frameworks is faster and easier than starting with generic reusable library. On the other hand, a framework will not be as generally useful outside the application domain because it contains domain-dependent components.

A framework comprises a set of components that express a design for a family of related applications. It is sometimes beneficial to adapt the developing software so that it fits to an available framework, resulting in a tremendous gain in productivity. Many other advantages come from the adoption of frameworks; in this aspect, several interconnected reusable components are more effective than a single universal library of components. Therefore, rather than creating a single library as a centralized repository of components, a better strategy is the development of specific reusable libraries for certain application domains.

4.3.2. Software Process Issues

The experience of using MOOD to design large and complex software systems has firstly shown that it is very difficult to follow either a strict top-down or bottom-up approach, and that it is necessary to switch over between them. This implies that it is helpful to clarify high level functionality for the software along with the identification of some low level objects and study their interactions. As a result, when developing large software, it is important to synthesize ideas from both top-down and bottom-up fashions.

One great advantage of applying object-thinking is the conceptual continuity across all phases of the software life cycle. Not only do the software concepts remain the same from system analysis down through implementation and maintenance, but they also stay uniform during the refinement of a design. Therefore, when object-orientation is employed, the design phase is linked more closely to the system analysis and the implementation phases because software engineers have to deal with similar abstract concepts (such as classes and objects) throughout software construction and evolution.

4.3.3. Mechanisms Prevalent in Each Life Cycle Phase

The most frequently used mechanisms in each phase of that life cycle model are pointed out in Table 4.2. These mechanisms are part of the abstraction process inherent to object-oriented software development as discussed earlier in Chapter 1.

Table 4.2: Phases versus abstraction mechanisms

Phases vs Mechanisms	System Analysis	Domain Analysis	Design	Implementation	Maintenance
Classification	√	√	√	√	√
Instantiation			√	√	√
Generalization		√	√	√	√
Specialization		√	√	√	√
Decomposition	√	√			
Composition		√	√	√	√

The system analysis phase emphasizes classification of high level concepts in a real-world application and decomposition of the software system. Several mechanisms are relevant to the domain analysis stage, but specialization, generalization and composition are vital to achieve reusability. In the design phase all mechanisms are fundamental as can be realized from the methodology steps. During the implementation and maintenance stages, almost all mechanisms are essential except decomposition, since at these latter phases the foremost partition of the software will have been done.

4.3.4. Percentage of Time per Each Development Stage

Although it is difficult to draw distinct lines between two adjacent software life cycle phases, Figure 4.5 indicates an approximate percentage of the amount of time likely to be spent on each phase for a complete development of a system. These statistics have been taken from the construction of a few software systems. Despite the system analysis, design and implementation phases being deeply interrelated, it is clear that the design phase takes longer because most of the tasks are done during this phase.

Domain analysis is relevant to figure out potentially reusable components during object-oriented software production. Consequently, the amount of time spent on this phase, naturally, must not be longer than that spent on other phases. If the perceived cost of finding a certain component is higher than the cost of creating a new component from scratch, then all hope for reuse is lost. For this reason, it is important to have at least minimal library tools which allow software engineers to select and add reusable components as they are identified.

Although maintenance accounts for the majority of software costs, it is not included in Figure 4.5 because it can be viewed as an operational phase which succeeds software development. It is felt that the basic reuse issues which MOOD encourages forms a useful basis for supporting software evolution, as it will be examined in great detail in the next chapters.

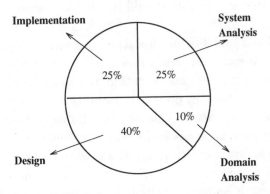

Figure 4.5: Phases versus software development time

4.4. Comments on the Software Process

The phases of the described software life cycle model are highly integrated. During the system analysis and domain analysis phases, user needs, software requirements, functionalities, objectives and constraints of the system are very much of interest. Thus, it is important to understand the real-world application, and an abstract model of that application should be achieved. When the design phase is entered, the abstractions are refined. The design process should stop when the key generic abstractions and the software behaviour are detailed enough to be translated into a programming language. Hence, the design phase generates the templates for the implementation stage.

Because experts tend to think in terms of high level abstractions, their prevailing tactic for software creation is top-down, whereas novices tend to follow a predominantly bottom-up fashion. When designers have good knowledge about the application domain, it is easier for them to divide the software into large components and think about high level abstractions. On the contrary, for those who have no previous knowledge about the application domain, it is better to rationalize in terms of low level abstractions, and instantiate some objects at that level to depict the overall software behaviour. In broad terms, it could be concluded that everything should be built top-down, except for the first time.

The top-down and bottom-up strategies have a significant effect on reusability because in a top-down manner reusability is mainly accomplished in terms of generalization and specialization of abstractions, whereas in a bottom-up way reusability is primarily achieved as aggregation of components. Therefore, following object-orientation, reusability not only becomes easier as a consequence of the traceability between real-world entities and its software counterparts, but it is also enhanced by mechanisms such as inheritance and composition.

Nevertheless, a software system is not merely produced out of reusable components. On the contrary, usually, components selected and derived from reusable libraries are combined with newly written components, and all of them have to be bound together in the final software. It is natural that with some of the components, the designer will face the decision of whether to reuse them straightforwardly, adapt them and reuse, or write them from scratch. The break-even-point of reusing versus redoing lies where the cost of search plus adaptation exceeds the cost of producing the respective piece of software.

Placing such arguments into an object-oriented software development picture, and particularly relating them to MOOD, produces the following observations. If the designer knows the application domain then it is easier to start up abstracting classes, finding commonalities between them, and building the class hierarchies. The use of the class hierarchy diagrams is quite appropriate for this activity. On the other hand, if the designer wants to begin a design by instantiating a few objects, then the object diagrams and operation diagrams must be utilized.

The implication of such observations on tools which automate software production, and specifically tools supporting a methodology is quite relevant. Designers should be aided by a whole range of tools. Tools indispensable at different stages of object-oriented development have been presented in Chapter 3. However, which tool is the most applicable to do a job, depends on the level of knowledge that designers have about the software being developed and on the application domain as well. Therefore, all tools should be made available to them at any time during software construction. They should pick up the tools that will help them deal with the concepts manipulated at a particular moment. By using a variety of tools, the designer is able to decide which one is the most suitable for each task. Consequently, a CASE environment should allow both bottom-up and top-down fashions to object-oriented software development.

Exercises

1. Based on your experience, do you reuse much software? If not, why not; if yes, how?

2. What are the major technical and non-technical factors which militate against widespread software reuse?

3. Estimate the additional time spent in turning an ordinary component into a reusable one and storing it into a reusable library.

4. Explain why reliability is so important to software reusability.

5. Is there any role for reusable libraries in the construction of rapid prototypes?

6. How does a reusable library affect object-oriented design?

7. Do automated tools promote software reuse?

8. Does designer's experience influence software reuse?

9. Why is the learning curve of reusable libraries usually steep?

10. Is it beneficial to draw a distinct line between object-oriented analysis and object-oriented design? Why?

11. What is the difference between object-oriented design and object-oriented programming?

12. Do system analysts need to know how to write programs? Should programmers be part of the design team?

13. What is top-down, bottom-up and middle-out software development?

14. When is object-oriented design characterized as a top-down, bottom-up or middle-out process? Which factors affect each trend?

15. Discuss how a methodology can take into consideration the designer's experience.

16. What factors determine software development time and costs?

17. How can managers estimate the human effort needed to produce a software system?

18. Draw a different chart that summarizes the phases of the presented software life cycle model, together with the deliverables at each stage.

19. How the use of proper tools change the way object-oriented software is designed? Does it have any influence in the software created?

20. "The object-oriented paradigm is a unifying model that can integrate all software life cycle phases seamlessly". Comment.

CHAPTER 5

SOFTWARE MAINTENANCE CONCEPTS

This chapter provides the general background on software maintenance and the necessary documentation, as well as introduces the software configuration management discipline to maintain legacy systems.

The first section of this chapter introduces the concepts, problems and categories of software maintenance. Section 2 concentrates on the current supporting maintenance technology. The documentation necessary to maintain legacy systems and the approach of incremental documentation are presented in section 3.

Section 4 looks at the software configuration management discipline, which has been applied primarily to the software development process, as another important factor in helping the maintenance of legacy systems. A brief summary of this chapter can be found in Section 5.

5.1. Software Maintenance Process

The IEEE[77] standard definition for software maintenance is given as:

> *The modification of a software product after delivery to correct faults, to improve performance or other attributes, or to adapt the product to a changed environment.*

Legacy systems [78] have been informally defined as:

> *Large software systems that we don't know how to cope with but that are vital to our organization.*

Software maintenance consists of a series of activities required to keep a software system operational and responsive after it is accepted and placed into production. In between, a variety of activities involving maintainers, quality assurance and configuration management personnel must be planned for, coordinated and implemented.

The current concern about software maintenance is that it is recognized as the most expensive phase of the software life cycle. In addition, the quality of code repairs and updates is often poor and this compromises the software system reliability and performance. Although many activities related to maintenance and development of software systems are similar, software maintenance has unique characteristics of its own, as detailed below:

- Software maintenance is performed on an existing software system. Any changes introduced to this system must conform to or be compatible with its architecture, design and code constraints.

- Software maintenance typically requires that programmers spend a significant proportion of their time attempting to understand how a program is constructed and how it functions.

- Software maintenance is usually open-ended, continuing for many years (as long as it is economically viable), in contrast to software development, which is undertaken within a timescale and to a budget.

- During software development, test data is created from scratch. Software maintenance can use this existing test data and perform regression tests, or alternatively, create new data to test only the changes and their impact on the rest of the software system adequately.

Software maintenance activities are commonly classified into four categories:

- `Perfective Maintenance:` enhancing the software system by altering its functional behaviour, which resulted from a change in the original intent or requirements.

- `Adaptive Maintenance:` changing the software system in response to a modification in the data environment (system input and output formats), or in the processing environment (either hardware or software).

- `Corrective Maintenance:` diagnosing and correcting errors which cause incorrect output or abnormal termination of the software system.

- `Preventive Maintenance:` updating the software system to anticipate future problems; this entails improving the quality of the software and documentation, or other software quality factors. Modifications in this activity do not affect the functional behaviour of the software system.

Not all modifications strictly belong to one category or another. For instance, corrective maintenance may also require enhancement (perfective maintenance) of a subsystem. Similarly, a subsystem may be redesigned to improve maintainability (preventive maintenance), due to the inability to correct a persistent fault in it.

Many problems associated with software maintenance can be traced to deficiencies in the way software systems have been defined and constructed. Lack of control and discipline in the initial phases of software development nearly always translates into problems during the maintenance phase. As this lack of control and discipline persists in the course of maintaining software systems, the structure and maintainability of such systems tend to deteriorate, often making them more complex and burdensome to maintain next time. The cost of failing to design software systems for maintenance is very high. Such systems become so fragile that maintainers and their managers are reluctant to change them. Any change may have unforeseen consequences, often causing problems in other parts of the system, annoying users and consuming precious software engineers time.

The necessity of performing software maintenance activities on a software system that has not been designed with maintenance in mind is arduous. Such a system is usually, for example, poorly documented, with an almost incomprehensible structure, and with the data representation embedded in the program code.

One consequence of this lack of maintainability during software development is loss of traceability, i.e. the ability to identify technical information which relates to a software error detected. Moreover, to make changes to a software system, maintainers normally need to understand the components of such a system, e.g. the contents and purpose of its modules, as well as the historical context in which the modules were developed. In legacy systems, such information is usually unavailable or out of date, and this situation deteriorates even more after maintenance is performed on those systems.

The net result of continual changes is that software systems tend to increase in size, and their structure tend to degrade with time. It has been said that the average program grows by 10% every year, doubling in size every seven years. Therefore, it is important to improve the maintainability of legacy systems in order to cope with its increasing lifespan.

It has been argued that new software development methodologies will reduce maintenance costs in the future. Nevertheless, it has also been shown that software systems must evolve if they are to continue to be useful, and thus, perfective maintenance will always be a vital activity. User enhancements account for 40% of all maintenance work, and only 20% is corrective maintenance. Furthermore, user demands for enhancements and extensions have been identified as the most crucial management problem area. Therefore, while new software development methodologies might reduce corrective maintenance, they will have little effect on the most expensive subtask, that is, perfective maintenance.

Another interesting observation is that most corrective and adaptive maintenance work is considered obligatory, while the other two types of maintenance (perfective and preventive) are mostly non-compulsory. Therefore, nearly half of all maintenance work is optional. From this, it follows that one way of minimizing the cost of software maintenance is to investigate perfective and preventive maintenance activities more carefully. Change request logs and formal change procedures are some schemes that may generate fewer and more thoughtful change requests, as can be seen in Chapter 6.

Currently, serious research into software maintenance tools and environments is being undertaken, but it is far less common than research into software development. Hitherto, no environments or tools have succeeded in integrating the diversity of maintenance tasks in a coherent way. Automated support is usually restricted to a single task of the maintenance process. There is a lack of automated maintenance support that could help maintainers during the whole software maintenance process, from change request to system release.

It is interesting to note that many projects concerned with software development claim that they will also assist maintenance. This is debatable as environments devoted to software maintenance have particular characteristics of their own. One such characteristic, for instance, is the capacity to capture the information of legacy systems into the environment. Various approaches to tackling such a problem are discussed in the next section.

5.2. Supporting Maintenance Technology

Legacy systems have not usually benefited from modern software technology which encourages good software engineering principles from the outset of software development. Hence, the use of software maintenance techniques, such as re-engineering, has been promoted as the answer to many of the problems of maintaining systems. The basic idea underlying re-engineering is that design information is extracted from the source code, so that it may be used to gain insight into the purpose of the software system, or to replace part or all of the system with modern software technology.

Re-engineering of software may be used for restructuring, extracting reusable components as well as providing new views of a software system and its documentation. The hope is that the maintainability and adaptability of legacy systems can be improved. The basis of all approaches to re-engineering is to try to make legacy systems easier to maintain. Unfortunately, re-engineering lacks a standard terminology and as such, different people often use different terms to cover the same basic concepts (and sometimes, the same names for different concepts). Attempts have been made in order to clarify terms such as reverse engineering, redocumentation, design recovery and restructuring [79], as they are described below.

Reverse Engineering

Reverse engineering is the process of analyzing a software system to identify its components and their inter-relationships creating representations of the software system in another form or at a higher level of abstraction in order to manage complexity. It is the part of the maintenance process which improves understanding of software systems and its structure, by giving a sufficient design-level view to aid maintenance, strengthen enhancement, or support replacement, given at worst the source code. Two sub-areas of reverse engineering widely referred to are redocumentation and design recovery.

Redocumentation aims to recover the documentation of a software system. It involves experienced programmers creating documentation by analysis of the source code as well as the recovery of useful documentation from the original documentation.

Design recovery recreates design abstractions from a combination of code, existing design documentation (if available), personal experience and general knowledge about the problem and application domains. It should reproduce the information required for a person to be able to fully understand a program; namely, what the program does, and how and why it does it.

Restructuring

Restructuring is the transformation of one representation form to another at the same relative abstraction level, while preserving the software system's external behaviour (functionality and semantics). It is often used as a form of preventive maintenance to improve the physical state of a legacy system, with respect to some preferred standard. It may also involve adjusting the software system to meet new environmental constraints which do not involve reassessment at higher abstraction levels.

5.2.1. Reverse Engineering Environments

Nowadays, available stand-alone tools, such as static analyzers and control flow restructurers, are increasing in number. However, these tools do not support any method for reverse engineering and are not designed to be integrated with other tools. Some projects, however, have the objectives of supporting methods and tools for reverse engineering, rather than simple restructuring functions. They cover a range of techniques, from simple control restructuring to design and specification recovery in preparation for new forward engineering. Nevertheless, the approaches adopted by these projects differ significantly.

Lano and Haughton [80] developed a method based upon the language Z++ to support the use of formal methods in software maintenance. The method is centered on the maintenance of the specifications and not upon the source code. Such formal specifications can be created, either from user requirements (forward engineering), or by reverse engineering an application. The abstract transformations are recorded during the reverse engineering process, building up the documentation. Change requests are translated and implemented into change requests to the specification, so that the application implementation can be generated together with revised documentation.

SOFTMAN

SOFTMAN [81] takes a different approach. Although it is designed to promote forward engineering, it also supports legacy systems by using reverse engineering. A noteworthy characteristic of SOFTMAN is that it assists in incremental verification and validation of software correctness across all life cycle activities. In SOFTMAN, a software system is correct if all of its life cycle descriptions are traceable, consistent and complete. Its method of maintaining legacy systems consists of importing them into the SOFTMAN environment to provide reverse engineering and subsequent forward engineering support. The same approach to reverse engineering is also being taken by other large projects in the area of software maintenance. Some of these projects are further discussed below. They offer a method together with a tool for reverse engineering, and they place considerable emphasis on a single integrated representation of the original software system in a system database.

REFINE

REFINE [82] is a tool for software maintenance which incorporates several technologies: an object-oriented database for source code and documentation and parsers for capturing and representing software; pattern languages for writing program templates and querying the database to find code that matches the templates; and transformation rules for automatically rewriting programs to meet new requirements. The query language based on templates for pattern-matching syntactic components empowers the maintainer to gather together all instances from the database that satisfy particular properties. This tool has been commercially used. For more complex systems, it allows its extension to meet special user needs by adding new capabilities.

REDO

The aim of REDO [83] is to assist software engineers in the maintenance, restructuring and validation of large software systems and their transportation between different environments. The objective is to articulate a theoretical framework for doing this and to develop the necessary methods and prototype tools. REDO is aimed, in the first instance, at the maintenance of Cobol data processing systems and scientific applications written in Fortran. The major focus and contribution of the REDO project is to provide a tool set for the reconstruction of software. The purpose of reconstruction is to take the software as it stands, and then to produce a more maintainable version. The REDO tools are integrated around a central database containing the application itself and all related information, including documentation and test data. A uniform user-interface to the toolkit has been developed. Applications are translated into an internal intermediate language, upon which the tools operate. The tools and methods are thus independent of the target languages, and may be applied to other languages by building suitable intermediate language translators.

MACS

MACS [84] (Maintenance Assistance Capability for Software) was a three year ESPRIT II project which addressed high level maintenance issues, and provided a maintenance assistance system in the form of a tool set. MACS covered the phases of reverse engineering, impact analysis and change management. It was intended to recover design specifications, given only source codes, so that functional specifications of the software could be recreated. From these, a new implementation of the application program could be achieved using up-to-date software engineering techniques. The MACS approach to software maintenance had three main characteristics. First, the design and structure of a legacy system was extracted using reverse engineering and was represented in a language-independent formalism called dimensional design. Second, the way in which software maintenance is undertaken was addressed by integrated front-end tools holding knowledge about the maintenance process and expert maintenance behaviour. The design of the user interface was strongly influenced by human factor analysis. Finally, the MACS system also attempted to capture design decisions and their rationale.

FermaT

The main objective of the FermaT [85] tool is to develop a formal specification from old source code. It is concerned specifically with reverse engineering legacy systems in order to bring them to a state in which modern software engineering techniques can be applied. The objective is to enable software, written in a low level procedural language (e.g. IBM 370 Assembler), be expressed in terms of non-procedural abstract specifications by applying formal transformations. The key feature of this process is the transformational approach: using a wide-spectrum language and verified transformations in order to simplify and abstract the low level source code.

All these projects use a common structure of a single repository in which all software items are stored, and where they are then accessed for manipulation by tools. All of them share the same presupposition, that a completely automatic approach to reverse engineering is impossible, though simple automatic tools can help at the tactical level.

Although REDO provides a contribution to the task of maintaining legacy systems, it lacks a discipline to control the reconstruction process of the software. It takes a top-down procedure to reverse engineering by focusing on the process and method, then implementing a tool set to support the method. Its key aspect is the integration of the tool set through the central repository.

The approach of MACS differs from the others as it provided automation through an expert system style, and offered an assistant tool, instead of a fully automatic tool set. It encapsulated knowledge about both the application domain and implementation, and the expertise of software maintainers. MACS provided some control for the reverse engineering process, since one of the layers presented in its architecture comprised a comprehensive configuration management system. Such functionality supported the changes during the maintenance process.

The approach of FermaT is yet different from the others, in that it consists of an interactive system for maintaining programs, which is based on program transformations. The transformations derive the specification of a program section, presenting the program in a different but equivalent form as an aid to program analysis and for general restructuring functions.

From the projects discussed in this section, it can be seen that the objective of the software maintenance environments is mainly reverse engineering legacy systems, to subsequently handing them over to forward engineering support. While reverse engineering may increase the maintainability of these systems, it may also incur unacceptable expenditure. When dealing with software systems having a predicted long maintenance life, this technique may be economically viable, but it seems unlikely to be appropriate for every kind of legacy systems. Therefore, alternative techniques to software maintenance still need to be explored, so that less expensive methods for maintaining legacy systems can be developed.

5.3. Documentation for Software Maintenance

Documentation is a critical and controversial issue in software maintenance. The Lientz and Swanson survey [86] identifies quality of software documentation as the most significant technical problem. The personnel close to software maintenance work perceives poor documentation as the biggest problem in this field.

Maintenance documentation provided by software engineers is, or should be, the major source of software information for maintainers. If the documentation is inadequate, the maintainer must use less convenient sources, or sacrifice the quality of the modification. This increases the risk of introducing an error, and causes software maintainability to deteriorate. The documentation should be accurate, usable and trusted by the maintainers. Outdated documentation is not only useless, but may also complicate and confuse the already difficult maintenance task.

Documentation has always been given a low priority status compared to other activities in software development. Documentation is nearly always left to the end of the project, and as software development invariably runs late, the amount of documentation originally planned is reduced, or even completely ignored. It is not unusual to find that the only documentation related to the design of a software system are comments within the source code itself. Moreover, software documentation is usually written by software engineers who do not necessarily understand the maintenance process. Therefore, document structure does not always provide enough visibility for maintenance purposes.

The controversy over software documentation is really concerned with the type of documentation required for maintenance, rather than the question of whether or not any documentation is needed at all. Not only the source code of software systems, but also their documentation must be maintainable. Producing voluminous amounts of detailed software documentation, requiring a major update effort each time a software component is modified, can only compound the maintenance burden.

Unlike the documentation that should be produced during software development, documentation for software maintenance does not mean the generation of a complete set of documents of a software system. As far as documentation is concerned, there are several differences between the processes of initial software development and software maintenance. In the initial stages of software development, there is more freedom in making implementation decisions. During most of this period, no source code is available, and there may be an imperfect understanding of how the software system should operate. In this case, the primary function of documentation is to make concepts clear and to communicate decisions. As for maintenance, there is considerably less flexibility. All design decisions must be integrated with the existing (and evolving) software system; both designers and users have a better understanding of their needs. Thus, at this stage, the documentation provides an abstract representation of the operational software system, which guides the design decisions that affect its evolution.

The most significant information required for maintenance is a description of what the software system does, and which software components cause it to do that. This depends heavily on a high level description of the structure of the software system which assists in locating specific information. Documentation should also explain why the users want the software system to do what it does, so maintainers can serve the real needs of users.

In addition, knowing how a software system has evolved during its development and maintenance is very useful information to the maintainer. Because the value of historic software development information has not been valued, it is rarely kept. However, it can greatly simplify the maintenance task. As well as clarifying user needs and development principles, this practice can help indicating the portion of the software system affected by particular decisions. Understanding the original design intention may guide the maintainer in the process of choosing ways to modify the source code that does not jeopardize software integrity and reliability. Also, knowing the parts of the software system that developers considered the most difficult may give the maintainer a first clue to where an error might lie.

Even within the maintenance process, documentation is not often produced, despite the maintainers' view that it is useful. Thus, the documentation, when carried out after the maintenance activity, is often inadequate in relation to the magnitude of the software change. The documentation of software evolution is an important aspect of software maintenance. Problem tracking and reporting are central to documenting software evolution. They are key aspects of recording changes to large software systems, which evolve over a long period of time and magnify the need for organized change tracking due to the number and extent of the changes made. Change histories provide important information about the reasons behind the changes to software systems. It has been found that more than 50% of errors and faults have been introduced by previous changes; the record of past changes is clearly a major contributor to software maintenance. Using these records, the original cause of failures can be traced, allowing the redesign of the original change, or at least, a better understanding of the cause of the problem.

In a more immediate sense, collection of data about the maintenance of a software system increases the visibility of the maintenance process and provides information to senior management. A record of changes (and the reasons for their institution) forms a permanent history of experience gained by maintainers.

5.3.1. Redocumentation

It is not always convenient to reproduce completely the design documentation from the source code, as it has not yet been established whether or not this is the most suitable documentation for software maintenance. In general, high level documentation explaining the overall purpose of the software system and describing the relationship of its various components is the most useful. Redocumentation for legacy systems can be a cheap yet effective productivity aid, especially when the process is undertaken incrementally and under a quality assurance procedure.

Many maintenance teams are forced into redocumentation because the documentation that is supplied with the software system they have to maintain is inadequate or nonexistent. One way of undertaking redocumentation is to reproduce the design documentation from the source code. Unstructured and inadequately documented software systems, which prove difficult to maintain, can be redesigned using modern programming practices. This technique is usually considered uneconomic on all but the smallest software systems. However, if this path is taken, it would be advantageous to use a documentation-support environment that manage the life cycle documentation set so as to have full control of the redocumentation process. These environments are primarily aimed at people designing new software systems, but they would also be of use in this approach to redocumentation. They enforce standards on the documentation and allow all the documents to be centrally located, providing easy access and updates.

Incremental Documentation

Since it may not be economically viable to reproduce the whole design documentation, it is important to identify techniques that allow redocumentation to take place gradually during the maintenance activity itself. If a redocumentation strategy for capturing the knowledge gained by maintainers while analyzing source code is to be set up, a number of key requirements should be stipulated.

One of these requirements is incremental documentation, i.e. the ability to build up documentation of a software system over a period of time in an incremental manner, without the need to document the complete software system in one step. This is an important requirement of a redocumentation strategy, as it allows the documentation to be produced as code is examined during the day-to-day software maintenance process, and not as an activity in its own right.

Another benefit is that only the source code which is analyzed by maintainers is documented. No time should be spent documenting source code that is in a stable state and may never be examined or modified. It has often been said that the 80/20 rule applies to software maintenance; 80 per cent of the time is spent on 20 per cent of the source code. Therefore, it is unproductive to document a complete system during software maintenance. Maintainers play a key role in this process by supplying information about the legacy system. The information they provide includes the various assumptions that are made during the implementation, and other semantic information that has not been recorded and is difficult, if not impossible, to obtain automatically with tools. By adopting this method, maintainers should be able to enter those details they judge to be important for the maintenance of a certain software system.

5.3.2. Support Available for Software Documentation

Over the past years a number of software documentation environments which support the production, management and use of textual and graphical documentation during all phases of the software life cycle have been developed. Most of these documentation environments promote traceability, central storage of all project documentation, easy access and update, and the enforcement of project-wide standards on the structure of documentation. The SODOS [87] and DIF [88] systems are examples of such environments; they concentrate on the production of conventional life cycle documentation during the development of a software system. Nevertheless, they are of little use to maintainers who are faced with a complete software system which has little or no existing documentation.

SODOS

SODOS [87] (Software Documentation Support) supports the definition and manipulation of documents employed during software development. It enforces standards on the documentation and allows the entire development documentation to be centrally located, providing easy access and updates. The SODOS system maintains a relationship between source code and its description, so that it is easy to go back and forth between them. Documentation in this form is likely to be a major factor in reducing the cost of software maintenance. Nevertheless, SODOS has limited use for the retrospective documentation of legacy systems during software maintenance. It would be necessary to redocument the whole system before any gains could be achieved in the maintenance phase. This is usually prohibitively expensive.

DIF

DIF [88] (Document Integration Facility) is a software hypertext system for integrating and managing the documents produced and used throughout the software life cycle. DIF departs slightly from other environments in that it has the additional aim of integrating documents within and across several projects into a single environment. Hypertext is used to provide traceability between life cycle phases (such as system analysis, design and implementation). Like SODOS, DIF manages life cycle documents in an object-oriented fashion. Its revision mechanism is limited to letting the user define the revision numbers for part of the documents stored.

In order to ensure that all the projects have a standard document structure, each document produced by DIF is defined as a form, which has a tree-structured organization of basic templates to be instantiated with project-specific information. Such forms provide a rudimentary way of defining the software process to be followed by the projects. DIF, however, does not provide the required support to redocumentation or to maintain legacy systems.

5.3.3. Documentation Tools for Software Maintenance

There are a number of tools available which claim to meet the documentation needs of software maintenance. The advantages of these tools are that they are inexpensive to operate and the documentation produced is easily kept up-to-date. Most of them take the form of static analysis tools, producing a series of reports. Examples of the documents generated are: control/data flow charts, cross-reference listings, metrics reports, call graphs and module hierarchy charts. All this information is of significant use to the maintainer when becoming familiar with the structure of a software system and in navigating around its components during maintenance investigations. What they fail to do is to provide any insight into why particular structures are used, or why certain design routes were taken.

This gap is bridged by the Rigi environment [89] which focus on structural redocumentation describing the system's architecture from multiple viewpoints. As human cognitive abilities are still more popular than hardwired algorithms, Rigi does not use a fully automated reverse engineering environment. This knowledge can only be recovered by eliciting information from the original designers, or by detailed examination of the source code by maintainers.

5.4. Software Configuration Management

Software Configuration Management [90,91] is an important element of software quality assurance. The purpose of the SCM discipline is to manage change throughout the software development and maintenance processes. Its primary responsibility is the control of change. However, SCM is also responsible for the identification of individual software configuration items and various versions of the software, the auditing of the software configuration to ensure that it has been properly developed, and the reporting of all changes applied to the configuration. It is a useful discipline to the project manager, allowing complex tasks to be executed in a well-organized way, and maximizing productivity by minimizing mistakes.

The SCM discipline has been defined by Bersoff *et al* [91] as:

> *The discipline of identifying the configuration of a system at discrete points in time for purposes of systematically controlling changes to this configuration and maintaining the integrity and traceability of this configuration throughout the system life cycle.*

In the SCM context, a software component is called a Software Configuration Item. A SCI is a part of the software system which is treated as a unit for the purpose of SCM. SCIs may be decomposed into other SCIs; they may also be modified, thus creating versions of the original SCIs. The range of SCIs which SCM must manage is very wide and includes source code, executable code, user and system documentation, test data, support software, libraries, specifications and project plans.

To provide management control, the concept of baseline is introduced. A baseline is the foundation of the SCM discipline. It is a defined state which SCIs pass at a specific time during their life cycle. The establishment of a baseline is generally carried out to indicate that the associated SCIs conform to some requirements or exhibit some characteristics. Before a SCI becomes a baseline, change may be made quickly and informally. However, once a baseline has been established, changes can be made, but a specific and formal procedure must be applied to evaluate and verify each change.

The Software Configuration Management discipline is considered to cover:

- *Version Control*, which identifies the SCIs and records the history of their evolution through successive versions.

- *Configuration Control*, which is concerned with the building of appropriately structured software systems from their constituent parts.

- *Change Control*, which deals with the operation of applying changes in order to establish new states the project goes through.

Although the SCM discipline is essential throughout the software life cycle, it is even more important during the maintenance phase. Software maintenance is concerned with changing legacy systems; SCM offers precisely the framework that is needed to manage such changes. Indeed, most software systems problems are often more acute during the maintenance phase when the largest number of SCIs, which exist in many versions and which are highly dependent upon each other, must be managed.

5.4.1. Functions of SCM

SCM does not stipulate a design method or life cycle model, nor does it define how the quality of items is to be judged. It does, however, provide a solid foundation for all other software engineering activities. SCM is the means through which the integrity and traceability of the software system are recorded, communicated, and controlled during both development and maintenance. This achievement is accomplished by the four main functions of this discipline which are: identification, control, status accounting and auditing.

Software Configuration Identification Function

Software configuration identification is a process that ensures meaningful and consistent naming for all items in the software configuration. This function exposes the constituent parts of a software representation in a manner which explicitly manifests the relationship among these parts. It is the process by which any piece of software is transformed into a structured entity. This SCM function supplies the mechanism for obtaining visibility and establishing traceability of the SCIs which comprise a baseline.

Software Configuration Control Function

This function is designed to respond to the need for change, but it also serves a more general purpose in the effective management of the software evolution. It stipulates the procedures necessary for proposing, evaluating, reviewing, approving and implementing changes to a baseline. Without these procedures, uncontrolled changes might cause more problems than they solve. All changes to a SCI should be controlled by using a formal procedure to obtain authorization to make the change. The body which authorizes change is usually known as a Configuration Control Board (CCB). The CCB must have the authority to evaluate proposals and authorize the implementation of changes to the software system. It is also a role of the software configuration control function to establish the standards for software development and maintenance, in order to prepare new baselines for review by configuration auditors.

Software Configuration Status Accounting Function

This function provides the mechanism and tools for recording and reporting the current status and evolution of a software system throughout its life cycle. This SCM function is satisfied when the outputs of the SCM identification, control and auditing functions are recorded, stored and can be reported.

Software Configuration Auditing Function

The purpose of this function is to increase the visibility of the software system and to establish traceability throughout its life cycle phases. A successful auditing should result in a baseline which checks that each to-be-established baseline possesses the appropriate technical relationship to existing baselines. The two fundamental processes within software configuration auditing are verification and validation. The verification process is largely an administrative function, while the validation process involves a technical assessment of the baseline. Verification entails evaluating software during each life cycle phase to ensure that it meets the requirements set forth in the previous phase. It ensures that the correct and current versions of all software parts are incorporated in the baseline, traceability to the previous formal baseline is included, and the software parts have the correct logical identification. Validation entails the evaluation of software at the end of each development effort to ensure that it meets its initial requirements. The maintenance validation involves regression tests, which help confirm the absence of unanticipated side-effects in functions not related to those being modified. It may also involve auditing the software system for adherence to design principles, implementation guidelines and other quality standards.

5.4.2. Automation of SCM

The SCM discipline has been widely employed and automated in recent years. The application of SCM throughout software development has shown to be an efficient method of improving both reliability and quality of the software produced. As recently as ten years ago, the discipline of SCM was considered of little value, mainly because it was performed manually. Therefore, project managers could not usually rely on the SCM organization because its performance was too slow and the work was error-prone.

In recent years, however, tools have been developed to automate the SCM process. Some of the first tools, such as SCCS [92] and RCS [93] deal primarily with source code versioning and storage. These tools offer good support for keeping track of versions of files in a software system, but provide only marginal support for understanding the structure of a large software system consisting of many modules, and for keeping track of relations between documents, source code and test cases.

Another tool named *make* [94], has emphasized the system-building aspects of SCM. However, *make* builds the software system using the latest versions of the files, with little regard for the previous versions. Several solutions have been proposed to integrate a version control system with a configuration management system, so that it would be relatively easy to identify and generate a specific version of a software system consisting of many modules. The integration of these two approaches is essential for the large and complex software systems currently being developed and maintained.

In small projects, the dominant aspect of SCM is the detailed recording of the who, what and when of each change made. To accomplish this, most projects use source-versioning systems. In larger software developments, however, communication and control become the dominant factors in managing change. There must be a set of well-defined procedures for reporting problems with the product, recommending changes or enhancements to the product, ensuring that all parties with an interest in a change are consulted prior to the decision to incorporate it being made, and ensuring that all affected parties are informed of the schedules associated with each change to the software systems. As a result, automated tools are considering the need to record, track and analyze volumes of data, and to maintain complex cross-references between large documents. Interactive tools have greatly reduced the amount of paper work. They enable SCM personnel to report accurate and timely information about the status of any requested change to any baseline to project managers.

Systems for configuration management and version control have evolved from simple stand-alone tools, such as *make* and SCCS, based on an underlying file system towards more integrated systems based on a project database. These tools and systems can be classified into three generations as follows.

The first generation tackled the problem of having two separate tools for performing the related tasks of SCM and version control. Although these tasks are integrated, they are not part of a software development environment. Moreover, these tools were working over unstructured text files. An example of tools from this generation is RCS working together with *make*. RCS, being primarily a tool for version control, offers a simple interface to *make*, in an attempt to integrate the activities of SCM and version control.

In the second generation, tools performing the related tasks of SCM and version control were integrated with the rest of the software development environment. The systems of this generation moved away from the file-system point of view, introducing the notion of a common database. One weakness presented by tools of this generation derives from the assumption that the employed programming languages have no constructs for inter-modular type-checking, and therefore have no means of expressing module interconnection. The consequence of this false assumption is that these tools require an external description of each component in terms of its import/export features and of the other components it uses. This approach is convenient when different programming languages are employed by different components, but it becomes an overhead in environments supporting languages which actually contain such constructs. This overhead consists of a lot of redundant information which has to be manually entered by the users.

The third generation tools are oriented towards high level languages. These tools take advantage of an underlying database, which provides a rich set of attributes that can be used for choosing the components needed to build up a software system. Another advantage of having a database as central repository is that the integration among different tools can be made very effectively. The tools classified in this category usually supply the mechanisms to enforce SCM policies, and automate the labour intensive clerical aspects of SCM, such as tracking and maintaining the historical information necessary for SCM status reporting and auditing.

From this brief analysis of the evolution of the application of SCM and version control, it can be seen that both SCM and version control should be performed within an environment, so that they can be integrated with other maintenance activities. A key aspect of this integration would be a database as the central repository of system knowledge and information, so that SCM and version control can be performed with reference to the conceptual schema underlying the environment.

5.4.3. Application of SCM to Software Maintenance

The SCM discipline has been used to improve the software development process with great success. Experience has shown that appropriate management can make the difference between project success and failure. By following sound management practices, developing projects can be kept on schedule, resulting in enhanced reliability, improving the quality of software systems produced and increasing job satisfaction. However, these same practices have not been applied to managing maintenance activities of legacy systems.

Traditionally, software maintenance has been treated differently from new development. Because it has been mistakenly viewed as less difficult and less important, maintenance has been often performed by less experienced software engineers under weak management supervision. The result is that management problems often outweigh the technical problems of performing software maintenance. Therefore, a management discipline which guides the maintainer through the maintenance process is of paramount importance.

The SCM discipline which is used to control software development can and must be used to control software maintenance, so that the task of maintenance does not cause the software systems to deteriorate after changes are introduced to them, and maintenance becomes more cost effective and reliable.

The automated support for the SCM discipline discussed in this chapter so far mainly deals with its application during software development. As far as software maintenance is concerned, few projects have been related to SCM. Such projects employ some aspects of the SCM discipline, for instance, the version control mechanism to allow specific versions of software components, such as specifications and test cases, to be retrieved; or deal with a particular software configuration function like the configuration identification function, and perform the first step aimed at regaining control over a legacy system. However, to improve reliability of a legacy system during its maintenance, traceability and consistency among the set of documents and source code should not only be established, but should also be preserved when changes to the source code are made.

5.5. Summary

This chapter provides an overview of the concepts of software maintenance, documentation for software maintenance as well as software configuration management. Additionally, this chapter has briefly surveyed a number of related automated support environments for software maintenance, and has outlined their strengths and oversights. The discussions in previous sections have also shown deficiencies in the current ways of tackling software maintenance. Good management of software maintenance is an achievable objective, but there is still inadequate technical support from methods and tools. Many tools in current use derive from the initial development phase, and are not well suited to the needs of maintainers.

The prominent software maintenance environments available are taking the approach of reverse engineering legacy systems, aiming at applying modern software development techniques to control their evolution. Incremental documentation, as discussed in this chapter, seems to be a viable strategy to incrementally recover the documentation of legacy systems while the maintenance process is being performed; concentrating only on those parts of the system which require modification, leaving the remainder alone. Furthermore, the software maintenance process would benefit if performed under the control of the SCM discipline. As a result, control over software systems would improve as maintenance is performed. The advantage of such a technique is that it is a less expensive alternative, by which the maintainability and documentation of software systems increase as they are maintained. Moreover, such a method can be routinely used to control the inevitable process of change.

Exercises

1. How do you feel about software maintenance? Would you enjoy doing it?

2. Why software maintenance cannot be neglected during the software life cycle?

3. Give some reasons why legacy systems cannot be just discarded despite the high cost to maintain them.

4. In which categories are software maintenance activities divided? Which category is mostly performed?

5. In which sense are corrective maintenance and debugging different?

6. Supporting maintenance technology is emerging. Give an overview of one of the software maintenance tools available and explain its importance to maintain legacy systems.

7. Explain why software documentation is important during software development and maintenance.

8. Software configuration management is an important discipline to be applied during software development. Explain why it should also be applied to software maintenance.

9. List some known tools which perform software configuration management functions. Describe to which particular software configuration function they are most appropriate.

10. Suggest some techniques and tools that you consider beneficial for maintaining legacy systems in a specific application domain.

11. "Redocumentation during software maintenance does not require the generation of a complete set of documents as necessary for software development". Comment.

12. "Software maintenance has been mistakenly viewed as less difficult and less important than software development". Discuss.

CHAPTER 6

SOFTWARE MAINTENANCE MODELS

As the size and complexity of software systems grow, so too will the maintenance burden, unless active measures are taken to plan for it and migration to software environments designed to minimize maintenance occurs. Imposing a structure onto the maintenance process of legacy systems may reduce the difficulty of the whole task by refining it to a number of tasks of reduced complexity. In order to structure the maintenance process, it is necessary to model it as in the software development process.

In this chapter, several models for improving software maintenance are analyzed, along with their advantages and shortcomings. Additionally, desirable capabilities of software process modelling are discussed in order to introduce the characteristics of software maintenance modelling.

6.1. Managing the Software Life Cycle with Maintenance

Because of the intangible nature of software systems, effective management relies on adopting models which make the software development process visible by means of documents, reports and reviews. This has resulted in the adoption of software life cycle models where the software development process is split into a number of phases and each phase is deemed complete when some deliverables have been produced, reviewed and accepted, as described in Chapter 4.

For sometime, the software development process has played a major role in the field of software engineering. During this period, the study of software processes has led to the development of various life cycle models that can be employed in the engineering of software. The basic function of a life cycle model in the development of a software system is to describe the chain of events required to create and maintain a particular software product.

The waterfall model is by far the most widely adopted software life cycle model. This model is typically high level and does not address detailed activities of the software life cycle. Although it suffers from inadequacies, it continues to be widely used as it provides several benefits to the software development process. Among the benefits of software life cycle models are the facts that they help software engineers to become aware of, and gain an increased understanding of the software process, and to determine the order of global activities involved in the production of software. These benefits may result in improved product quality, increased effectiveness of methods and tools, reduced software development and maintenance costs, and increased user and software engineer satisfaction.

Despite some variations, the main phases of a traditional software life cycle model are: specification, design, implementation and maintenance, with possible feedback loops between phases. The current view of the software life cycle, however, mainly emphasizes the development phases. It does not portray the system life, i.e. it does not show the evolutionary development which is characteristic of most software systems, only showing the creation and development of a system. The traditional waterfall model has always shown the software maintenance activity as a single phase at the end of the cycle. This final phase needs to be replaced by a model which reflects the aspects of software evolution. What is required is a new, broader perspective of the software life cycle, emphasizing change, maintenance and migration to new technologies. On the basis of the discussion so far, this final phase should also break the work to be done into tasks or stages which can be performed in such a way that the quality-cycle concept can be used to control the quality of the software maintenance stages and the individual tasks; progress can then be reviewed at the end of each stage.

6.2. Existing Software Maintenance Models

It is now quite common to divide the software development process into separate phases. Similar models have been proposed for software maintenance. A software maintenance model describes the individual steps necessary to satisfy an individual maintenance request. Different types of maintenance requests, environment characteristics, and budgetary constraints may require different models.

One of the causes of many maintenance problems is the lack of good maintenance models. Practical software maintenance models tend to be more *ad hoc* and are performed without easy access to the necessary information. In addition, the maintenance technology level (i.e. methods for design and code reading, and automated tools) is much lower than for software development. The result of all the above is unproductive and error-prone maintenance.

A number of authors have proposed models for software maintenance. The software maintenance models described in this section outline basic guidelines and phases which, as the authors suggest, are to be followed during the maintenance of legacy systems. These models have been proposed in the last two decades and have slightly evolved to keep up with new technologies that have emerged. They have been divided into three separate sections to show their evolution, reflecting the chronological order in which they were developed. Accordingly, the first models are typically high level, giving only general guidance, and not addressing detailed activities of the maintenance process. The recent ones, though also high level, introduce more advanced software engineering principles.

6.2.1. Early Software Maintenance Models

The early models of software maintenance were very simplistic. They provided the order of phases to be followed, without addressing the details of how they should be performed. The Boehm [95], Liu [96] and Yau and Collofello [97] models are representative of these early software maintenance models.

Boehm Model

Boehm outlines three major phases of a maintenance effort in his model. However, he does not detail the exact maintenance tasks within each phase. The three phases of the Boehm model are:

1. Understanding the existing software.

2. Modifying the existing software.

3. Revalidating the modified software.

Liu Model

The significance of the legacy system is highlighted in the model devised by Liu. Unfortunately, he does not provide any details regarding the tasks within each of the phases of his model either. The Liu model consists of a high level, general model which comprises three phases:

1. Understanding of the capacity, function and logic of the existing software system.

2. Designing of new logic to reflect the new request or additional feature.

3. Merging new logic with existing one, so that the new logic is integrated into the existing software system.

Liu puts forward some suggestions to improve the documentation of legacy systems and stresses its importance for software maintenance. The documentation, however, is not part of any of the phases of his model. Liu also emphasizes that strict testing procedures should be followed, although a testing phase is not itemized in his model.

Yau and Collofello Model

The Yau and Collofello model identifies four basic phases in managing the software maintenance process. Their model focuses on software stability through analysis of the ripple effect of software changes. These activities can be accomplished in the four following phases:

1. *Understand the program.* Consists of analyzing the program in order to understand it.

2. *Generate a maintenance proposal.* Consists of generating a particular maintenance proposal to accomplish the implementation of the maintenance objective. This requires a clear understanding of both the maintenance objective and the program to be modified.

3. *Account for ripple effect.* Consists of accounting for all of the ripple effects as a consequence of program modifications.

4. *Testing.* Consists of testing the modified program to ensure that it has at least the same reliability level as before.

Each of the four phases are connected to software quality attributes. The first phase is associated with complexity, documentation and self-descriptiveness attributes, which contribute to ease the understanding of a program. In the second phase, the way of generating maintenance proposals for a program is affected by the attribute extensibility. Yau and Collofello state that one of the most important quality attributes is the stability of the program (in phase three), because if the stability of a program is poor, the impact of any modification on the program is large. In the fourth phase, the primary factor contributing to the development of cost-effective testing techniques is the testability of the program.

6.2.2. Middle Software Maintenance Models

The models described in this subsection are better elaborate than those in the previous one. Martin and McClure's model [98], for instance, discloses further details on how to perform the task of maintenance; while Patkau's model [99] explains detailed functions to be performed according to the maintenance category. Arthur's model [100] is more comprehensive, providing guidelines for the change request to system release phases.

Martin and McClure Model

The high level breakdown of the tasks clarified by the Martin and McClure model is similar to that offered by other investigators. The three basic phases are:

1. *Understand the program.* This entails understanding the functional objective, internal structure and operational requirements of a program. This function is subdivided into three subfunctions:

   - Top-down understanding. A top-down approach should be used to become familiar with a program at a general level of understanding, then at detailed level.

   - Improve documentation. During the understanding of the program, document what is learned, concentrating on improving high level program documentation.

   - Development participation. When possible, participate in the program development process to learn about the program.

2. *Modify program.* This involves creating new program logic to correct an error or to implement a change, incorporating that logic into the existing program. It requires the following substeps:

- Devise a plan for changing the program. A top-down strategy is recommended to review the program. First, the modules and data structures to be changed are isolated. Next, the internals of each module and data structure to be changed are studied in detail. The change is then designed, specifying the new logic and any existing logic that must be altered.

- Alter the program code to incorporate the change. The objective of this step is twofold: to correctly and efficiently code the change, and to eliminate any unwanted side effects from the change.

3. *Revalidate the program.* The maintainer should perform selective retesting to demonstrate that not only is the new logic correct, but also that the unmodified portions of the program remain intact and the program as a whole still functions correctly. The maintainer should:

- Test for program failure by performing system tests to be sure that the entire system is still operating correctly as a whole.

- Test the unmodified portions of the program by performing regression tests to determine if those parts still operate correctly.

- Test the modified portions of the program to determine if the changes were designed and implemented correctly.

Patkau Model

A more comprehensive approach to software maintenance is presented by Patkau. He first presents a generalized high level model which identifies five basic maintenance phases. His model is then further refined, and four versions of the generalized model are presented.

Each of these versions models the four categories of software maintenance: corrective, perfective, adaptive and preventive maintenance. An important feature of this model is its emphasis on specification and localization of the change. The five phases of the Patkau's model are:

1. Identification and specification of the maintenance requirements.

2. Diagnosis and change localization.

3. Design of the modification.

4. Implementation of the modification.

5. Validation of the new system.

The refined versions of the generalized model differ in the first two phases. The remaining phases of the model are similar among each of the four categories of software maintenance. Although Patkau preaches further refinement of these phases, they will not be discussed here as they are similar to those of previous models.

For perfective maintenance, the two initial phases are:

1. Identify new or altered requirements, and specify operation of the enhanced system.

2. Locate affected elements.

For adaptive maintenance, the two phases are:

1. Identify a change in the environment. Describe the change and revise specifications to reflect it.

2. Locate the elements affected by the change.

For corrective maintenance, the first two phases are described as:

1. Identify repeatable error symptoms and specify correct operation of the system.

2. Locate the part of the system responsible for the error.

For preventive maintenance, the two first phases are refined to:

1. Identify a deficiency in performance, maintainability, etc., and specify desired performance or quality standard.

2. Locate the source of the deficiency.

Arthur Model

Arthur proposes a more elaborate and comprehensive model for software maintenance. His model presents phases to deal with the request for changes until they are implemented, tested and released to the users. The seven phases of his approach to tackling the software maintenance process are:

1. *Managing change.* The basic objective of change management is to identify, describe and track the status of each requested change. In this phase, change requests are generated and analyzed.

2. *Analyzing change.* The overall objective of impact analysis is to determine the scope of the requested change as a basis for planning and implementing it. Change requests are evaluated for potential impact on existing systems, other systems, documentation, hardware, data structures and humans (users, maintainers, and operators). A preliminary resource estimate is developed.

3. *Planning system releases.* The principal objective of system release planning is to determine the contents and timing of system releases. Change requests are ranked and selected for the next release. Changes are batched by work product, and the work is scheduled.

4. *Designing changes.* The major objective of the design phase is to develop a revised logical and physical design for the approved changes. Logical design relates to the system level, and physical design relates to the program level.

5. *Coding changes.* The objective of coding is to change the software to reflect the approved changes represented in the system (logical) and program (physical) designs.

6. *Testing changes.* The primary objective of testing is to ensure compliance with the original requirements and the changes approved.

7. *Releasing the system.* The objective of system release is to deliver the software system and update documentation to users for installation and operation.

6.2.3. Recent Software Maintenance Models

The recent models dedicated to software maintenance are illustrated in this section by the Foster [101], Pfleeger [102] and request-driven [103] models. While Foster's model tries to approach maintenance from an organizational viewpoint, Pfleeger's model is an attempt to improve the maintenance process by managing it through metrics. The request-driven model attempts to portray the activities of software maintenance as dictated by user requests for change involving strict control from management.

Foster Model

Foster *et al* argue that the organization of software maintenance is of critical importance to the success of the activity itself. Their model is derived from the observations made by actual maintenance teams and covers technical and managerial issues. This model differs from others discussed in this chapter in that it does not dictate the phases to be followed during the maintenance process, but refers to the functions (duties) performed by people involved.

The model specifies the four following functions which are triggered by queries, problem reports and change requests sent by users.

1. *Front desk* receives these communications from users and retains records of them. It is the responsibility of the front desk to

provide answers/solutions, either directly or by passing on the request to a more specialized team.

2. *Request store* receives the requests which demand new solutions. The request is queued until effort becomes available. This queue is represented as the request store, which contains a backlog of unactioned requests. The management of the request store is an important function. Priorities are assigned among its contents, and preliminary investigations and impact analysis are performed in order to plan future work. If the preliminary investigations reveal that the team does not have the resources or capability to answer a problem, a request must be made to some other team to come up with a solution. If that team can cope with the request, it will be dealt with as one of a repeated series of actions, in which the highest priority request is taken from the store and the software change designed.

3. *Change store* accumulates changes and solutions received from other teams. From time to time, a decision is taken to build a new release of the software, incorporating all new changes available.

4. *Solution store* provides a set of known answers/solutions which are accessed by the front desk. This represents information in a variety of forms, such as versions of software products and paper records of answers to frequently asked questions. If the solution is in the store or can be quickly generated, then it is immediately solved and issued back to the user. New solutions are also lodged in the solution store, from where they are available for distribution to the original users.

Pfleeger Model

Pfleeger describes a model for software maintenance which emphasizes impact analysis and forms a framework for software maintenance metric support. The model incorporates metrics for assessing and controlling change. Pfleeger's model can be seen as an improvement on that of Yau and Collofello, as the software quality attributes are connected to the phases so as to monitor product quality. The major activities of this model are:

1. *Manage software maintenance.* This controls the sequence of activities by receiving feedback with metrics and determining the next appropriate action.

2. *Analyze software change impact.* It evaluates the effects of a proposed change. If the impact of the change is too large, or if traceability is severely affected by the change, management may choose not to implement the change.

3. *Understand software under change.* Source code and related product analysis are needed to understand the software system and the proposed change. The likely degradation of system characteristics, such as complexity of the system, self-descriptiveness of the source code and documentation quality, helps to decide if the change will be implemented or not.

4. *Implement maintenance change.* This generates the proposed change. Adaptability of the system is analyzed to perceive the difficulty of implementing the change.

5. *Account for ripple effect.* This analyzes the propagation of changes to other modules as a result of the change just implemented. Stability, coupling and cohesion of affected modules serve to check the original impact analysis effectiveness.

6. *Retest affected software.* The modifications are tested to meet new requirements, and the overall software system is subject to regression testing to meet existing ones. Testability, completeness and verifiability are observed in this activity.

Request-driven Model

The request-driven model portrays the activities of software maintenance as dictated by user requests for change. The model consists of the following three major processes, which involve strict control from management:

1. Request control.

2. Change control.

3. Release control.

The *request control* process deals with the user's requests for change. The major activities which take place during this stage are:

- Collection of information about each request.

- Setting up of mechanisms to categorize requests.

- Use of impact analysis to evaluate each request in terms of costs and benefits.

- Assignment of a priority to each request.

Change control is often seen as a key process, the most expensive activity being the analysis of the existing code. The activities involved in this process are:

- Selection of changes from the top of a priority list.

- Reproduction of the problem (if any).

- Analysis of code, documentation and specification.

- Design of changes and tests.

- Quality assurance.

It is during the *release control* stage that requests to be included in a new release of the software system are decided and the necessary changes to the source code made. The activities which take place during this process are:

- Release determination.

- Building of a new release by editing source, archival and configuration management, and quality assurance.

- Confidence testing.

- Distribution.

- Acceptance testing.

The software maintenance models discussed in this section provide a means of communication between the personnel involved in the maintenance task, assistance in the management, and some may lay a foundation for building maintenance-driven tools. However, because these models offer mainly high level guidelines, they do not present sufficient details of actions and events necessary to ensure the quality and maintainability of software systems which should precede each new release. Existing maintenance models still lack a framework with rigid guidelines, in order to make certain that legacy systems are improved rather than impaired after each change is introduced.

6.3. Software Process Modelling for Maintenance

Models for software development, as is the case for most of the software maintenance models described in the previous section, represent the software development process in terms of phases. On the other hand, software maintenance models characterize the maintenance process from the maintainer's perspective only. The structuring of maintenance activities provides a useful mechanism for improving the process. However, the application of these models has been of limited benefit in actually aiding the maintenance process. Moreover, existing models do not describe the actual processes which occur during software maintenance; they may only provide a means of visualizing the process in terms of interim products. Phase milestones could be associated with these products, thus providing a mechanism by which management satisfaction could be assessed with respect to general requirements, budgets and schedule.

Moreover, software maintenance models, like software development models, should provide wider aid to fully encompass the whole process. Software process modelling can be defined as a methodology that embodies a representation approach, comprehensive analysis capabilities and the ability to make predictions regarding the effects of changes to a process. Several diverse goals and objectives have been cited as motivation for the development and application of software process models. These include support for automated execution and control, human interaction (such as execution guidance), various management responsibilities, process understanding and analysis of processes.

Thus, a software maintenance process model can be defined as the specification of a systematic approach to the maintenance of software. With the purpose of extending the experience and technology of software development process to software maintenance, four primary objectives for the development of software process models should be outlined as follows:

1. Enable effective communication, regarding the process to others (managers, software engineers and users).

2. Facilitate reuse of the process by enabling a specific software process to be instantiated and executed in a reliably repetitive fashion across multiple software projects.

3. Support evolution of the process by serving as a repository for modifications, lessons learned, tailoring, and by analyzing the effectiveness of changes in a laboratory of simulated environments before actually implementing them. Successful tailoring decisions should then be formalized and stored as part of the model, so that they can be consistently applied in the future.

4. Facilitate effective planning, control and operational management of the process. This is accomplished through increased understanding, training, conformity to process definitions, quantitative simulation and analysis capabilities, and definitions and use of measurements and metrics.

In order to accomplish these objectives, software process models must possess capabilities in three major categories:

- A powerful representation formalism is required to cope with the complexities of actual organizational processes.

- Comprehensive analysis capabilities, including a wide variety of tests in the areas of consistency, completeness and correctness. They are critical in determining the validity of the model itself, and of the actual process the model represents.

- Forecasting capabilities which can be provided through simulation that is tightly integrated with the model representation and analysis features.

From these observations, a list of numerous desirable capabilities for an ideal approach to software process modelling is presented below.

1. Use a highly visual approach to information representation, such as graphical notations.

2. Enable compendious descriptions, i.e. comprehensive in scope, yet concise in presentation.

3. Support multiple, complementary perspectives of a process, such as functional, behavioural, organizational and conceptual data modelling.

4. Support multiple levels of abstraction (e.g. hierarchical decomposition) for each perspective.

5. Offer a formally defined syntax and semantics, so that the constructs are computable.

6. Provide comprehensive analysis capabilities. This would involve tests in categories such as consistency, completeness and correctness.

7. Facilitate the simulation of process behaviour directly from the representation.

8. Support the creation and management of variants, versions and reusable components of process models.

9. Support the representation and analysis of constraints on the process, such as regulations, standards and so on.

10. Enable the representation of purposes, goals, rationales, and so forth, for process components and the overall process.

11. Integrate easily with other approaches which may be deemed useful.

12. Take an active role in process execution.

13. Offer automated tools supporting the approach.

Techniques for software process modelling are still under research and the availability of even a portion of the requirements described above is expected to bring substantial benefits to the software development and maintenance processes. Besides, these requirements may in the future, facilitate the evolution of software processes in a methodical and disciplined fashion.

6.4. Characteristics of Software Maintenance Modelling

Hinley and Bennett [104] argue that process models need to have the following characteristics in order to provide real benefits for maintenance management:

- A comprehensive coverage of the software maintenance process, but avoiding complexity.

- A large scope addressing organizational, behavioural and functional aspects.

- Recognition of real-world objects by the model (change requests, fault log).

- Recognition of explicit roles of the people (manager, maintainer, user) who interface with the maintenance process.

- A suitable diagrammatic form, so that measurement and control points can be established.

- Recognition of the process communication pathways, which may not reflect an activity sequence or organizational hierarchy, e.g. management control mechanisms.

- A framework which guides managers in their use; for instance, how they can measure process performance against stated goals, with the aid of a maintenance model.

- Reusable features, for example, supply of process modules or templates which can be refined or tailored to suit individual maintenance project circumstances such as the change request control process and the change release process.

- Flexibility so that models can be quickly adapted to cater for real process transformations and changing relationships.

The requirements for software process modelling for maintenance, in addition to the characteristics for maintenance management described above, have been analyzed in order to lay a basis for comparison with the software maintenance model to be described in the next chapter. The proposed model encompasses most of the desirable capabilities necessary to generate a supportive maintenance process. Additionally, it provides aid for maintenance management, as detailed below:

- It covers each maintenance activity from change request to its release to users.

- The objects of the formalization are real-world elements such as change proposal, maintenance specification and configuration release.

- It considers the people involved in the maintenance process as well as their roles.

- The functional process model provides a diagrammatic form of representation which allows measurement and control points to be established.

A relevant aid for the management of the maintenance process is the functional process model, which defines the framework necessary to systematize the software maintenance process, by specifying the chain of events and the order of stages that a change has to go through. This model:

- Comprises ways of coping with the need and justification for changes.

- Improves the flow of maintenance activities by providing guidance throughout the maintenance process.

- Provides a formal change control procedure to monitor changes and protect software quality.

- Determines the organization and content of the information needed to support the maintenance activities.

6.5. Summary

In this chapter, a survey of software maintenance models has been presented. Although there is a relatively large number of software maintenance models, they have displayed oversights which require further research into this field. Relevant characteristics of software maintenance modelling have also been discussed, in order to introduce the necessity of generating alternative approaches to improve maintenance of legacy systems.

Exercises

1. Software life cycle models for software maintenance have already been used for some time. Give some reasons stressing their importance and weaknesses.

2. Are the existing software maintenance models playing any role during the maintenance of legacy systems?

3. What are the main differences between software maintenance models and software life cycle models?

4. Describe the features of a software maintenance model that you judge useful. Explain your answer.

5. Which of the software maintenance models presented in this chapter would be most applicable for maintaining your software systems? Why?

6. Do you think that software systems developed using a spiral life cycle model are likely to be difficult to maintain? Why?

7. In which aspects the recent software maintenance models are better than the early ones?

8. Which other features would you include in the current software maintenance modelling in order to improve it?

9. "There should be various software maintenance models to suit several application domains". Comment.

10. "Many people argue that the activities associated with software maintenance are not maintenance at all, thus the term *maintenance* is incorrectly applied to software". Discuss.

CHAPTER 7

MAINTENANCE OF LEGACY SYSTEMS

The previous chapters presented some aspects of the maintenance of legacy systems. Various existing models for software maintenance have been discussed and their strong points and drawbacks have been pointed out. Despite increasing recognition that maintenance is a major problem during the life cycle of software systems, there are still diverging opinions about how to tackle this problem. This chapter presents a generic methodology for software maintenance named **COMFORM** (COnfiguration Management FORmalization for Maintenance). COMFORM will be used in this book to introduce further software maintenance concepts.

7.1. Objectives of COMFORM

COMFORM [105] aims to provide guidelines and procedures for carrying out a variety of activities during the maintenance process by establishing a systematic approach to the support of legacy systems. The methodology accommodates a change control framework around which the Software Configuration Management (SCM) discipline is

201

applied. It exerts control over an evolving software system while simultaneously redocumenting it in an incremental fashion.

The application of the software configuration management discipline (SCM) is central to the COMFORM methodology since this discipline is concerned with the use of a set of procedures and standards for managing evolving software systems. In essence, it is concerned with change: how to control change, how to manage software systems which have been subject to change, and how to release these changed systems to the users.

COMFORM does not attempt to change programs in order to fix an error or to implement a modification, but it aims at improving the future maintainability of legacy systems while being maintained. Without the application of the SCM discipline, it is easy to release a wrong or bad version of a software component. A primary goal of applying this discipline to the methodology is to improve the ease with which changes can be accommodated, thereby reducing the amount of effort expended on maintenance.

The major activities carried out by COMFORM are:

- Acceptance of change proposals and analysis of their viability for implementation.

- Enforcement of evaluation of approved changes in terms of costs and resources.

- Promotion of scheduled system releases, so that the maintenance process can be planned and organized.

- Specification of the maintenance task by grouping together the modifications of a system release.

- Provision of technical and managerial reports.

- Enforcement of documentation of software components which require modification.

- Enforcement of the application of software quality by assuring completeness and consistency of legacy systems.

- Provision of audit trails as well as historic and current status of changes.

- Provision of guidelines for revalidating legacy systems.

- Provision of input to project management and quality assurance systems.

A change control framework has been established in COMFORM in order to preserve software quality. The Software Maintenance Model institutes this framework, which aims to systematize the software maintenance process by specifying the chain of events and the order of stages that a change has to go through. The output of the SMM phases are represented by forms which allow a methodical approach towards the establishment and control of traceability throughout the maintenance process. These forms are the source of documentation of maintenance history and system redocumentation. The use of the SMM forms results in considerable advantages, such as:

- Provide a uniform structure of documents of software systems under COMFORM, since forms are pre-defined. Such a uniformity of information avoids inconsistency and unnecessary differences.

- Facilitate the application of SCM techniques, since it is easier to control pre-defined documents.

- Ease completeness checks, by ensuring that no essential details are omitted.

- Ease consistency checks, by certifying that the information required by a form is provided by other forms in a configuration.

- Facilitate traceability between phases by establishing the relationships between components of different phases in the forms.

This chapter concentrates on the methodology underlying COMFORM. Therefore, the SMM framework is presented, followed by the forms which represent the outcome of the phases. The role of the

SCM discipline, and each of the SCM functions, as they relate to COMFORM, are also discussed.

7.2. Software Maintenance Model

The Software Maintenance Model targets at improving the flow of maintenance activities by providing guidance throughout the maintenance process, and determining the organization and content of the information needed to support these activities within COMFORM.

SMM identifies the activities undertaken during software maintenance and the information needed or produced by these activities, supplying a framework around which quality assurance activities can be built in a purposeful and disciplined manner. Being a maintenance model, the SMM highlights the considerable influence of the existing software system on this whole process. The outcome of each SMM phase is a completed form which represents a point in the maintenance process. These complete forms are, therefore, the natural milestones, i.e. the baselines of the software maintenance process, and offer objective visualization of the evolution of that process.

The following phases comprise the SMM:

1. Change Request

2. Change Evaluation

3. Maintenance Design Specification

4. Maintenance Design Redocumentation

5. Maintenance Implementation

6. System Release

Figure 7.1 portrays the SMM. In this figure, the rectangles represent the SMM phases and the ovals indicate the baselines formed from the output of the phases. Being a software maintenance model, it is essential that the influence of the evolving software system on the process should be examined. For this reason, the *change evaluation* phase has been introduced, during which modifications are considered in relation to the existing software system. The need to understand legacy systems is motivated by the information required by the incremental redocumentation process. Understanding will be facilitated by the information contained in the SMM forms as changes take place.

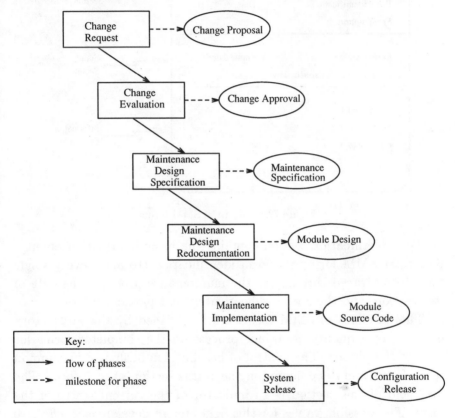

Figure 7.1: Software Maintenance Model (SMM)

Like models of software development, SMM phases may overlap. Also, it may be necessary to repeat one or more phases before a modification is completed. However, the products which represent the output of the phases must constitute a baseline, and cycling must be controlled. The output of SMM phases is a number of pre-defined forms which consist of three sections (*identification*, *status* and *infor-*

mation), as depicted in Figure 7.2.

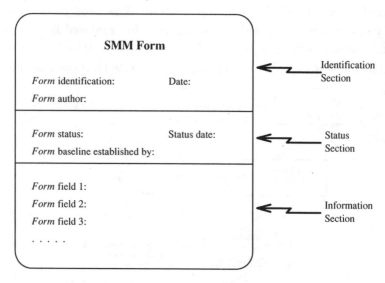

Figure 7.2: Pattern of SMM forms

The *identification* section contains the basic information about a particular SMM form: the form identification (to allow every single form to be traced throughout the maintenance process), the date of its creation, and the author who created that particular form.

The baselines of SMM forms are established by the satisfactory outcome of a quality assurance process on the completed forms for each of the phases. The control of baseline establishment is common to all forms and documented in the *status* section of each form. The first field of this section is an indicator of the current status of the form. The possible values for this field are: *in development*, *effective* and *frozen*. The initial status of the forms is *in development*. The status changes to *effective* after its initial evaluation. The final status of a form is *frozen*, when its baseline is established. The second field records the date on which the current status has been assigned to the form. When the status of the form is *frozen*, the last field records the author who established the baseline.

The *information* section is specific to each SMM form and contains data concerned with particular phases of the model. The fields of this section will be detailed subsequently, as the following subsections of this chapter give further details of each particular phase.

7.2.1. Change Request

All requests for software maintenance is presented in a standardized manner. A form named `Change Proposal` (CP) is the one associated with this SMM phase. The filling in of a `change proposal` form triggers the process of maintenance in COMFORM. The form contains the basic information necessary for the evaluation of the proposed change. If the proposed change is for corrective maintenance, then a complete description of the circumstances leading to the error must be included. For the other types of maintenance, an abbreviated requirement specification must be submitted. Figure 7.3 shows the basic information for any type of change proposal.

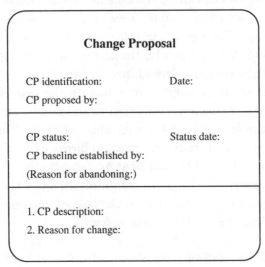

Figure 7.3: `change proposal` form

While the information contained in the *identification* section of this form was described earlier in this chapter, the *status* section for this particular form incorporates one additional field: *Reason for abandon-*

ing. The *CP status* field is an indicator of the status of the proposed change in the maintenance process. The initial status is *in development* when the change is assigned for evaluation. That status changes to *effective* after its initial evaluation. The final status is *frozen* when the change proposal may have been approved and a corresponding change approval form has been generated in order to carry on the change evaluation. The proposed change may also be rejected (which will also be *frozen*), and is then followed by filling in the field *Reason for abandoning.* The field *Status date* shows the date the current status has been assigned to the form. Where the status of the form is *frozen*, the author is associated with the *CP baseline established by* field.

In the *information* section, the field *CP description* provides a short functional or technical description of the proposed change, so that it can be evaluated and then approved or rejected. The field *Reason for change* is a brief description of the benefits of carrying out the change. This is used to help the maintenance staff to rank and approve the proposed change. The justification for corrective changes for the most part is straightforward. Usually, the change will be made on the justification that the program must function correctly. However, in some cases, the cost of the change or its effect on the rest of the software system may be so enormous compared to the minor inconvenience resulting from the failure that the user may choose to tolerate the failure rather than risk introducing new problems or modifying present operating procedures. The justification for adaptive, perfective and preventive changes may be more complicated, since the benefits may be difficult to evaluate compared to the cost of implementing and the risk of degrading the quality of the software.

7.2.2. Change Evaluation

In the *change evaluation* phase, the maintainer is primarily concerned with understanding the change, and its effect within the software system. An accurate change diagnosis is performed to assess the feasibility of the proposed change in terms of cost, resources, and schedule, resulting in approval or rejection. The rejected proposed change is then abandoned. If the proposed change is approved, a corresponding `Change Approval` (CA) form is created and its evaluation continued. The inadequacies, or unfulfilled requirements described in the `change proposal` form are identified in the existing software system. In addition, every software component involved in the proposed change must be known. If the information contained in the `change approval` form is comprehensive then maintainers are able to react quickly to problems, analyze enhancements properly, evaluate impacts and estimate resources. In this phase, the approved changes are ranked and selected for the next system release. The changes are batched by system releases and the work is scheduled. The result of this phase is the `change approval` form depicted in Figure 7.4.

The `change approval` form is one of the documents used as a basis for planning the system release. It is a vehicle for recording information about a system defect, a requested enhancement and quality improvements. The `change approval` form, along with its corresponding `change proposal` form, is the basic tool of a change management system. By documenting new software requirements or the ones that are not being met, these forms become the contract between the person requesting the change and the maintainers who work on the change. The field *Related CP* ties the `change proposal` form to its corresponding `change approval` form.

The field *Type of change* classifies the work as perfective, adaptive, corrective, or preventive maintenance. The information contained in the field *Identification of change* shows the maintainer something about the nature of the work as well as indicates to management how maintenance time is going to be spent. This field provides a more elaborate functional and technical description of the approved change, which is dependent on the type of maintenance as outlined below:

- `Perfective Maintenance` - Identify new or altered requirements.

- `Adaptive Maintenance` - Identify the changes in the environment.

- Corrective Maintenance - Identify repeatable error symptoms.

- Preventive Maintenance - Identify the deficiencies in performance, maintainability, etc.

Change Approval

CA identification: Date:

CA authorized by:

CA status: Status date:

CA baseline established by:

---

1. Related CP:

2. Type of change:

3. Identification of change:

4. Involved sw components id.:

5. Resource estimates for change (design):

6. Resource estimates for change (coding):

7. Resource estimates for change (testing):

8. Priority of implementation:

9. Consequences if not implemented:

Figure 7.4: change approval form

The field *Involved sw components id.* reveals information about which software components are directly involved in a change. The ripple effect of a proposed change is necessary to estimate accurately the scope of work and the resources required. Once the impact and ripple effect of a change are determined, preliminary resources estimates can be calculated. These estimates are approximations of the work required to accomplish the changes in all the involved parts of the software system. Estimates can be expressed in any unit of measurement meaningful to the organization, such as hours, days or weeks. The fields *Resource estimates for change*, which apply to design, coding and testing, record these resource estimates for a proposed change. Such estimates are important to project management and can also be used as references for similar work on other projects, or future system releases.

The field *Priority of Implementation* indicates the time frame necessary for completion of the task. This classification is important as it highlights the magnitude, criticality, or complexity of change proposals. The priorities are classified as:

1. *Critical* - Where repairs should receive immediate attention ahead of any currently scheduled system release.

2. *Important* - When the software system is operational and can be manually overridden or ignored until a specific date. The proposed changes may upgrade to *critical* priority if the problem is not fixed by the required date.

3. *Minor changes* - When the proposed repairs and enhancements can be deferred until the next system release, but time and resources permitting, should be performed for this release.

4. *Optional* - Includes slight repairs or enhancements that may be worked out in the next system release, as resources and time allow.

Critical approved changes should be attended immediately by the maintenance staff. Other changes may be collected for periodic review by a configuration control board. This board includes user representatives as well as members of the maintenance organization. The responsibilities of the board include deciding the fate of change proposals based on long-term goals of the organization, user needs, cost considerations and the batching of approved changes by system releases. Before being reviewed by the board, change proposals are studied by the maintenance staff to determine the resources (effort and time) needed to make each change, the impact of the change on other software components, and the cost of the change. The field *Consequences if not implemented* is then filled in by the maintenance staff during this preview analysis, in order to provide more information to the board.

7.2.3. Maintenance Design Specification

This phase is characterized by the structure of the modification, which is in the form of a complete, consistent and comprehensible common specification of all changes that should be made. In addition, how the software components have to be modified is clarified. All the related approved changes selected for the next system release will be in the same maintenance specification. The design of a modification requires an examination of the side effects of changes. The maintainer must consider the software components affected, and ensure that component properties are kept consistent. The integration and system tests (to be performed during the revalidation process in the *system release* phase) need to be planned or updated. In addition, if the changes require a new logic or new features to be added to the system, then these have to be specified and incorporated. In this phase, the activities to be performed are detailed, in order to figure out the alterations necessary to implement all the related approved changes (which have been batched for the next system release).

The boundary between the *change evaluation* and the *maintenance design specification* phases may at times seems blurred, because the analysis and review performed in the *change evaluation* phase sometimes overlap with the specification of the changes. Nevertheless, this phase is more concerned with generating a common specification for all changes proposed and approved for a planned schedule release. The resultant form for the *maintenance design specification* phase is the Maintenance Specification (MS) form, represented in Figure 7.5.

The maintenance specification form is generated after the approved changes for the next system release have been selected. The relationship between these selected changes and their corresponding specifications are detailed in the field *Related CAs* of the created `maintenance specification` form. In the specification of the proposed changes, the different types of maintenance require diverse ways of specifying the changes. The field *Specification of change* should take these differences into account as described below:

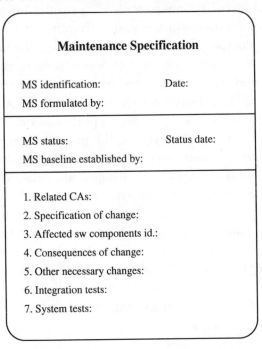

Maintenance Specification

MS identification: Date:
MS formulated by:

MS status: Status date:
MS baseline established by:

1. Related CAs:
2. Specification of change:
3. Affected sw components id.:
4. Consequences of change:
5. Other necessary changes:
6. Integration tests:
7. System tests:

Figure 7.5: `maintenance specification` form

- `Perfective Maintenance` - Specify operation of the enhanced system.

- `Adaptive Maintenance` - Revise the specification to reflect the change and adapt the original specification to the new system environment.

- `Corrective Maintenance` - Define correct operation of the software system.

- **Preventive Maintenance** - Establish the desired performance or quality standard and/or redesign a distinct subsystem to satisfy the same specification, so that it uses less resources, or is better structured and maintainable.

The field *Affected sw components id.* provides information about which software components are indirectly affected by the proposed changes. Such components often come out during the impact analysis of the proposed changes. In the case where several software components are affected by these changes, resources estimates may have to be reviewed and the schedule for the next system release be updated.

The field *Consequences of change* reports the side effects encountered during the impact analysis of the proposed changes. The optional field *Other necessary changes* may have to be filled in if, during the specification of the approved changes, unpredicted changes have to be performed in the software system in order to fulfil the original proposed changes. For instance, if during the impact analysis, the proposed changes affect software components not predicted in the analysis and review, new change proposals have to be elaborated and introduced to the formal change control procedures established by COMFORM. In such instances, this field is filled in by clarifying the relationship between the current maintenance specification with new `change proposal` forms.

Tests plans should be elaborated at this stage. They should be based on impact analysis and describe how and when the software system should be tested. The fields *Integration tests* and *System tests* should contain the tests to be carried out in the software system in order to complete the next system release. For instance, during the integration tests (with unit test completed) only the interfaces between the modified software components need to be examined, whereas during the system tests, only the interfaces between users and the modified software components require checking.

7.2.4. Maintenance Design Redocumentation

This phase, along with the next SMM phase, facilitates system comprehension by incremental redocumentation. The purpose of the forms associated with these two phases is to document the software components of a legacy system under COMFORM. Therefore, the forms are filled in when the corresponding software components have to be modified. The software components that should be changed are redefined and the new components which might appear must be specified.

The algorithms and behaviour of procedures for both normal and exceptional cases are also explained in this phase. Additionally, the tests for each of the changed or implemented software components are planned. The form connected to this phase is named `Module Design` (MD) form, as depicted in Figure 7.6. The information contained in this form is independent of the maintenance category being performed.

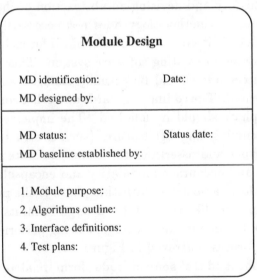

Module Design

MD identification: Date:
MD designed by:

MD status: Status date:
MD baseline established by:

1. Module purpose:
2. Algorithms outline:
3. Interface definitions:
4. Test plans:

Figure 7.6: `module design` form

COMFORM proposes a one-to-one relationship between a `module design` form and an existing software component. The purpose of such a relationship is to capture a higher level documentation of these components, while maintaining them. The aim of the `module design` form is to produce some documentation to enhance readability and to convey more clearly the software component meaning. Thus, the field *Module purpose* contains an outline of the purpose of the software component linked to that `module design` form. In the *Algorithms outline* field the limitations, restrictions and algorithmic idiosyncrasies of a software component are recorded. The current input and output interfaces of a software component are kept in the field *Interface definitions*. Unit test plans should be elaborated in this phase and kept in the field *Test plans*. During unit test, only the revised software component and the specific changes need to be examined.

7.2.5. Maintenance Implementation

One of the purposes of COMFORM is concerned with building up maintenance history and devising an abstraction of the evolving system. Therefore, the methodology does not necessarily deal directly with the source code itself. In this phase, SMM forms have a link with the components of an existing software system. This is the phase in which the source code should be actually changed and new components implemented. The coding standards and other conventions specified for this phase should be followed. The implementation should exploit programming language features (such as structuring facilities, user-defined types and assertion statements) to state properties and dependencies, and encourage modularity and encapsulation.

The SMM form associated with this phase is the `module Source Code` (SC) form, and like the `module design` form, its information is independent of the maintenance category being performed. A `module source code` form is portrayed in Figure 7.7.

There is one `module source code` form related to each software component and a one-to-one relationship between each `module source code` and `module design` forms. The information contained in each of these forms complements the other. The field of the `module source code` form (*Corresponding MD*) explicitly links the forms of

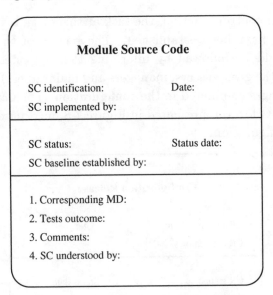

Figure 7.7: `module source code` form

these two phases. While the `module design` form is aimed at keeping general and stable information for a software component, its corresponding `module source code` form retains the information pertaining to modifications performed in these components. Hence, the field *Tests outcome* records the result of the unit test performed after a software component has been modified. Further, the field *Comments* may contain any remark detected during the implementation of the modification which is worth documenting. The last field, *SC understood by*, records the name of the maintainer who has some knowledge about that particular software component.

7.2.6. System Release

System release is the last phase of the SMM before a new configuration holding the approved changes is released to the users. Validation of the overall software system is achieved by performing the integration and system testings on the system.

Once modifications on the system have been performed under the configuration control function, the task at this stage is to certify that all baselines have been established. The release of the new configuration should be followed by informing the interested and related members of the group (users, managers and maintainers) about the requested changes completed in the configuration. The `Configuration Release` (CR) form, represented in Figure 7.8, incorporates details of the new configuration.

Configuration Release

CR identification: Date:

CR created by:

CR status: Status date:

CR baseline established by:

Comprises:

CPs:

CAs:

MSs:

Is composed of:

1. Integration tests outcome:

2. System tests outcome:

3. Configuration distributed to:

Figure 7.8: `configuration release` form

A `configuration release` form is the system release planning document, which embraces the information pertaining to the history of a maintenance phase. The fields *Comprises CPs, CAs* and *MSs* are concerned with retaining the connection to the `change proposal`, `change approval` and `maintenance specification` forms which constitute that particular system release. A `configuration release` form also shows the `module design` and `module source code` forms that have been modified during that particular system release. Such links are displayed in the field *Is composed of* at the end of the development of the corresponding `configuration release` form. Additionally, in order to release the system to users, the integration and system tests must be performed. The outcome of such tests should be documented in the fields *Integration tests outcome* and *System tests outcome* respectively. The successful outcome of these tests enables the `configuration release` form to have its baseline established. The users who will receive the current system release are registered in the field *Configuration distributed to*.

7.3. SCM Discipline Applied to COMFORM

In the previous section, SMM phases have been described. The emphasis was on the description of each type of form and their fields, together with their respective meanings and functions in the COMFORM methodology.

The specific functions which the SCM discipline plays in the whole process are detailed in this section. The SCM discipline provides the formal mechanism to establish the baselines of the methodology. Such baselines can only be changed through the formal change control procedure. In the following subsections, details of the application and guidance indicated by the four functions of the SCM discipline on COMFORM are described.

7.3.1. Software Configuration Identification

The purpose of this function is to highlight the constituent parts of a software system in such a way that makes explicit the relationship between these parts. It is the process by which the pieces of an existing software system are transformed into a structured entity, hence identifying the Software Configuration Items (SCIs). Therefore, this is the first function which should be executed in COMFORM so that the SCM discipline can be applied to the whole maintenance process determined by the methodology. The SCIs in COMFORM have already been identified and defined as SMM forms. The effect of this function is to provide the structure of links and dependencies between the forms. It also helps during the task of obtaining the components involved in, and affected by, a required change. As a result, the SCM discipline is able to control the release and changes in the forms throughout their existence, record and report their status, as well as verify their completeness and consistency.

7.3.2. Software Configuration Control

The software configuration control function in COMFORM is concerned with the control of changes made in a legacy system, from the change proposal, evaluation, approval and implementation, to its release. It is also concerned with the establishment of standards for software maintenance. Therefore, in the context of this book, its role is to ensure that any change required in a legacy system is defined and implemented by following the SMM phases, which institute a change control procedure to monitor changes. In so doing, change information is gradually recorded by the filling in of forms. This procedure ensures that all work performed to implement a change is traceable to change proposal and that changes to a software system can only be made by properly authorized maintainers. It also prevents unauthorized changes from being made, since no implementation can proceed without authorization. As changes are traceable to the original change proposal, the auditing process can check that only the approved requested changes have been made in the software components. This SCM function also controls the versions of SMM forms. The version control in COMFORM is further detailed in the next section.

7.3.3. Software Configuration Status Accounting

The objective of the configuration status accounting function is to record and report the current status, as well as the evolution of legacy systems. The information necessary to perform this function is incrementally obtained while the SMM forms are filled in as a result of changes to the software system. The implementation and effective use of this function in COMFORM is achieved by its automation and by the supporting information contained in the SMM forms.

A number of reports can be obtained in order to answer a variety of queries about the legacy systems kept under COMFORM. Such reports can be of help either to project managers or maintainers, by showing information such as productivity, or providing the history and current status of a software system.

Typical queries about the software's managerial aspects could be:

1. Which software systems are under COMFORM?

2. How many system releases of a particular software have been created?

3. What is the number of change proposals made per software component?

4. What is the number of change proposals made per maintenance category?

5. How many and which software components are being modified per maintainer?

6. What are the total resources spent on incorporating a particular change proposal in a system release?

7. What are the total resources spent on designing, coding and testing each maintenance category of a specific software?

8. Which `module design` forms have been documented by a certain maintainer?

9. For each `module source code` form, which maintainers understood the software component?

10. What are the change proposals requested by a special user?

11. Which users have taken delivery of a particular system release of the software?

12. How many change proposals are outstanding on a specific software?

On the other hand, typical queries involving technical aspects which help maintainers are:

1. How many change proposals are grouped in a certain system release?

2. What are the creation and release dates, and the status of a system release?

3. Which change proposals are related to a particular software component?

4. Which module design forms are incomplete (not *frozen*) in a specific system release?

5. How many times has a software component been changed (number of versions) and what are the reasons for these changes?

6. Which forms are related to a particular system release?

7. What is the current status of the system configuration to be released?

8. Which change proposals of a certain software system have been rejected?

9. Which maintenance specifications are related to a certain software component?

10. What is the system configuration released on a special date?

11. What are the versions of a distinct software component?

7.3.4. Software Configuration Auditing

The traditional SCM auditing function comprises the processes of verification and validation. The verification process is largely administrative, basically consisting of performing checks on the outcome of phases, in terms of correspondence and traceability to the previous baseline. It ensures that the correct and current versions of all software components are included in the baseline. The validation process involves a technical assessment of the baseline, i.e . validating it against the change proposal requirements. It may also involve regression tests to investigate the absence of unanticipated side effects in functions not related to those being modified.

The auditing function within COMFORM is the process which determines the overall acceptability of the proposed baseline at the end of each SMM phase. This process establishes the baselines of SMM forms. It uses the related product assurance disciplines of test and evaluation, completeness, consistency and quality assurance.

The auditing process in COMFORM can be divided into two separate stages. The first stage basically consists of performing checks on SMM forms for the completeness and correctness of the information. The checks are specific to each SMM form, and consequently differ from one SMM form to another. The outcome of the software tests which have been performed are also examined at this stage. The aim of the second stage is to establish the baselines of all forms involved in a system release; thus, consistency and traceability between SMM forms are checked. Further details of these two stages are given next.

Initial Evaluation

The basic checks performed during the first stage are dependent on each SMM form. The result of this phase alters the status of the forms from *in development* to the intermediate status *effective*. In order to upgrade the `change proposal` form, the proposed change should be evaluated and the decision, whether it should be implemented or abandoned, must be taken.

The checks applied to the change approval form require that the proposed change must be clearly understood and identified by pointing out the software components involved in the modification, as well as stating the resources estimates, schedule and priority of implementation.

In the *maintenance design specification* phase, a maintenance specification form should provide a complete, unambiguous and comprehensible specification of all the changes of a system release. In addition, the integration and system tests must be elaborated and other necessary changes (if any) should also be included in the maintenance specification form.

At this stage, the module design forms must be filled in, thus assuring that the documentation of the software components, which have undergone modifications, is improved. Additionally, the individual tests of those software components should be specified. This phase may also involve the simulation of the software design, in order to validate the software system with the end users or to check for requirements which are not covered by the current change design.

During the *maintenance implementation* phase, it must be assured that individual tests of the modified or newly implemented software components are performed to investigate their functionality and interface standards. Furthermore, checks that the coding standards are in compliance with the standards defined by the software configuration control function must be made.

In the *system release* phase, checks should ensure that the integration tests which exercise the modified functions or subsystems have been performed. These tests should be carried out independently and in controlled combinations. Checks should also make certain that system tests have been executed, to verify that the software system meets its specified requirements. Additionally, the use of correct versions included in the system release to be completed must likewise be verified.

Establishment of Baselines in COMFORM

The establishment of baselines is the most important step to be carried out at the end of each SMM phase. Baselines are established from the successful outcome of the application of quality assurance procedures to the SMM forms. The result of this stage alters the status of the forms from *effective* to the permanent status *frozen*.

Establishment of baselines is performed after the initial evaluation of the auditing process, and represents the moment when all the consistency and traceability checks have been performed. The essence of this stage is to examine, not individual forms, but the overall set of SMM forms, which represents a system release. Therefore, this process has a sequence which should be followed, in order to make certain that the specified forms are in accordance with each other, and to assure the integrity of data being manipulated during a system release.

The first stage of the process of establishing the baselines is represented by the `module source code` form, since it is the form which links the software component to COMFORM. Therefore, to have their baselines established, the forms of this category must be documented and be in accordance with the corresponding software component. The second stage of establishing the baselines involves the `module design` forms, which represent a higher level of documentation of those software components.

The documentation of the maintenance process is obtained from the `configuration release`, `change proposal`, `change approval`, and `maintenance specification` forms. As a result, the sequence by which the baselines are established should follow the sequence of SMM phases. Hence, the `change proposal` form is the first one to have its baseline certified, which means either the `change proposal` form has been approved and the maintenance process should be carried on, or the proposed change should be abandoned after having been rejected. The consistency check enforces the one-to-one relationship between an approved `change proposal` form and its corresponding `change approval` form.

The `change approval` and the `maintenance specification`

forms should be filled in independently of each other, but obviously the change approval form has its baseline established first. Such events only happen if the corresponding forms of the involved and affected software components have already had their baselines certified. After this point, it is presumed that the implementation has already been carried out, so the next step involves the final evaluation of the system release. In this case, the configuration release form should be filled in with the results of the testing and have its baseline established.

At this point, the new system release is ready to be made available to the users, with the assurance that all the software components required for maintenance activity have been documented, and that the maintenance applied to the software system has been monitored and controlled.

7.4. Version Control in COMFORM

Legacy systems usually have many different versions and consist of large numbers of software components, which in turn may have several different versions. It is useful to keep track of various versions of these systems, as well as the versions of the software components which make up a particular release of such systems. COMFORM supplies this capability by providing a mechanism to manipulate versions of SMM forms, and to enforce restrictions on the evolution of such forms, so that this evolutionary process is observable and controllable.

Two types of versions can be distinguished: *revision* and *variation*. COMFORM adopts both concepts, but a version (revision or variation) of a form is only created after undergoing the quality assurance process (defined to establish the baseline) of the corresponding SMM phase. Hence, a version of a form is under SCM control, and it can no longer be changed. If other changes to this version are required, a new version should be created.

A *revision* of a form is a new version, created to supplement previous ones. A form may have many revisions, reflecting its evolution. Each successive revision should denote the removal of existing software errors (corrective maintenance), the improvement of earlier revisions by either adding functionality (perfective maintenance) or improving the quality of the software being maintained (preventive maintenance). Consequently, revisions are in a linear order, being related to the time sequence in which they are created.

A *variation* of a form fulfils a similar function for slightly different situations and therefore acts as distinct versions for the same form. Multiple variations of a form may coexist as equal alternatives. Unlike revisions, there is no meaningful linear order among variations. The intent of creating variations is to support coexistent alternatives, such as different types of hardware (adaptive maintenance) and alternative functionalities (adaptive and perfective maintenance).

All versions of a form are related to each other by being either revisions or variations. There may be both variations and revisions of a single form, as a variation may require software error corrections and performance improvements, resulting in multiple revisions of a variation.

Since versions represent the satisfactory outcome of the quality assurance process of SMM forms, other ways of controlling their evolution before they are under SCM control need to be adopted. For this reason, SMM forms can be in one of the three groups: *in development*, *effective* or *frozen*. A version of a form (revision or variation) is obtained when its status is *frozen*. Therefore, before reaching the *frozen* status and being under SCM control, they are called *alternatives*. Alternatives have to be developed and audited in order to reach the *frozen* status. When alternatives are being developed, their status is *in development*. At this stage, maintainers can make as many modifications as required to the fields (from the *information* section) of the alternatives. Once the development or modification of an alternative has been completed, its status becomes *effective*. At this point, modifications to this alternative cannot be made and the quality assurance procedures are applied in order to perform the SCM auditing function. The successful outcome of the application of such procedures generates a version of a form, whereas its failure returns the alternative to *in development* status to allow the necessary changes to be performed.

The SMM forms which are first created during a system release are called *original* SMM forms. These are produced as a result of the formal procedures established by COMFORM, having their baselines established at the end of a system release. Once baselines have been certified, the forms representing them cannot be changed. If modifications are required, alternatives should be created and controlled. Such alternatives are generated according to the *versioned* SMM form, which is portrayed in Figure 7.9.

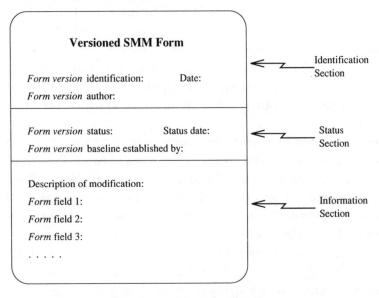

Figure 7.9: Versioned SMM form

A versioned form (like an original form) also contains three sections termed *identification*, *status*, and *information*. The *identification* and *status* sections of a versioned form are very similar to the original form, except for the fact that they contain information about an alternative/version. Every versioned form for all types of SMM forms has an additional field in the *information* section. This field is called *Description of modification,* and its content documents the purpose of generating an alternative for a particular *frozen* form. The remaining fields of the *information* section for every versioned form are the same as those for the corresponding original SMM forms described earlier.

The necessity to create versions of forms is demanded by modifications required to them after they have been *frozen*. In COM-FORM, SMM forms do not receive the same treatment, as far as version is concerned, since their purpose in the methodology is different. That is, the `change proposal`, `change approval`, `maintenance specification` and `configuration release` forms are aimed at documenting maintenance history, whereas the `module design` and `module source code` forms purpose is to provide an abstraction of the running software system. Thus, the concepts of *revision* and *variation* are more suitably applied to the latter forms.

A `change proposal` form may have versions if it was once *abandoned*. In this case, the generation of a version allows abandoned change proposals to be put back into the software system. A `change proposal` form may also have a version in case of discrepancies being found during its evaluation; consequently, corrections are required to be undertaken by the person who proposed the change.

`Configuration release` forms may also have versions. The intention of a version of a `configuration release` form is to link configuration releases which are either dependent on each other or part of the same context. This concept allows, for instance, the creation of a version of a `configuration release` form to correct errors in the previous releases. In doing so, the set of versions of `configuration release` forms provides the history of the system release evolution.

Versions of `change approval` and `maintenance specification` forms should only be created to correct inconsistencies generated during their implementation. Therefore, versions of `change approval` and `maintenance specification` forms will only exist within a system release. Once a `configuration release` baseline has been established, versions of its `change proposal`, `change approval` and `maintenance specification` forms can no longer be generated. New modifications to them mean the creation of a new `change proposal` formwith its corresponding change approval and maintenance specification forms generating an extra configuration release form.

On the other hand, as module design and module source code forms are the means of documenting software components, they may have various revisions and variations to reflect the system evolution. The semantics of the required change determines whether a revision or a variation of the module design and module source code forms should be created. It is during the *change evaluation* phase that such a decision has to be made. In the case where a proposed change requires the replacement of module design and module source code forms, a *revision* of them should be created. However, if the proposed change is intended to act as an alternative to the existing module design and module source code forms, a *variation* of them should be generated.

7.5. Remarks on COMFORM

A model for software maintenance has been presented in this chapter, initially without reference to versions. The relationship of the model to the SCM discipline has been examined and later the issue of versions has been introduced.

In broad terms, the application of COMFORM starts when a change to a legacy system is proposed, and finishes with a new system release to the users. Between these two stages there are phases which guide the maintainer throughout the software maintenance process. These phases are covered by the SMM, with the aid of the corresponding forms for each of its phases. The SMM has been put forward to improve the flow of maintenance activities.

The SCM discipline applied to COMFORM provides the mechanism for maintaining and controlling the various baselines throughout the development of the forms which constitute a system release. In essence, SCM embraces the whole change process. Hence, the application of this discipline contributes directly to software quality by identifying and controlling changes, assuring that changes are properly implemented, and reporting changes to interested people.

Exercises

1. It may seem odd that costs and schedule estimates are taken into account during the change evaluation phase before the mainte-nance design specification phase has been conducted. Why do you think this should be done this way? Are there circumstances when it should not be performed?

2. Make an estimate of the cost of carrying out maintenance in a particular legacy system that you know well.

3. Explain the importance of the process of establishing baselines during the development and maintenance of software systems.

4. Discuss the differences between the verification and validation processes of COMFORM. Why validation is more complex than verification?

5. What is the importance of the maintenance design specification phase? Suggest other fields you judge relevant to the form connected to this phase.

6. Suggest software maintenance techniques and tools which could be useful in assisting ripple effect analysis of a proposed change.

7. In which sense can maintenance history be helpful during the software maintenance process?

8. Which fields would you add to the change approval form to maintain a large and complex software system? How does it depend on the kind of change or type of maintenance?

9. How do you estimate the effort, in terms of time, that is required for a certain change to be implemented in a software system?

10. Recall a software system that you developed in the past. How difficult is it to add new functionality to that system? Is it maintainable?

11. Prepare a documentation for a program that you wrote some time ago. Have you found any difficulty in redocumenting the program now?

CHAPTER 8

OBJECT-ORIENTED SOFTWARE EVOLUTION

This book has concentrated on object-oriented design and maintenance of software systems. The purpose of this final chapter is threefold: firstly, to show how object-orientation can be applied to software maintenance; secondly, to provide final remarks on the development of object-oriented software; and finally, to present further thoughts concerning object-oriented software design and maintenance as well as the future of object-oriented software engineering.

8.1. Object-Orientation for Software Maintenance

Until recently software maintenance has been the neglected phase in the software engineering process, despite the fact that maintenance of legacy systems may account for over half of all efforts expended by a software organization. The percentage continues to rise as more software systems are produced. Furthermore, as legacy systems age more effort is likely to be expended on maintenance.

Therefore, the realization of maintenance as the core in the development and continued utility of software systems has become more widespread. This change in attitude has come from the recognition that the emphasis on short-term goals of creating a software product in the shortest time (to succeed in a competitive market) with low priorities being given to quality or to long-term sustenance of the product, has been very costly to the software industry.

Nowadays, competent software engineers often seek to develop systems which have extended lifetime. Besides, the advent of object-orientation opens up the technical possibility of effective reuse of software. Hence, there is greater economic justification for considerable effort to be spent on making a software component reusable (in many respects this is equivalent to making it maintainable) since this component may have many users and a prolonged lifespan.

Reusability built upon the mechanisms of inheritance and composition should be of great concern during software development; being domain analysis an adequate framework to encourage it. The exploitation of reusable libraries is a major plus for productivity, despite the overhead costs to develop generic and robust components. In the long-term, software reusability principles should be extensively applied, so that the knowledge of an application domain can be reused as skeletons for similar applications in the same domain. On top of that, the overall economic impact of reuse on maintenance and re-engineering [106] is as important as its effect on software development.

As it has been presented in previous chapters, the purpose of the software maintenance methodology COMFORM is to provide guidelines and procedures for carrying out a variety of activities during the maintenance process; this is accomplished by establishing a systematic approach to support legacy systems. It has been observed that it is almost impossible to come up with a software maintenance environment which can be applied to maintain all sorts of software systems at the same time satisfying the needs of all maintainers. One way of solving such a problem is defining specific software maintenance environments to cover certain kinds of systems. Another alternative is to create a strategy which allows flexible parameterization in a software maintenance environment, so that the environment is able to attend the needs of the maintenance of diverse software profiles.

In this section, a software maintenance environment which takes the latter approach is put forward. Thus, it concentrates on describing the application of object-oriented thinking together with the software maintenance methodology COMFORM. The merge of these two approaches results in a software maintenance framework generic enough to let software managers capture and reuse maintenance knowledge within specific application domains, so that a wide range of software systems can be maintained [107].

8.1.1. Definition of SMM Forms Using Class Hierarchies

A class is the main concept for a software maintenance methodology that follows an object-oriented fashion. Its definition is carried out by the software manager before starting the maintenance of a legacy system. Each SMM form of COMFORM is mapped by a class specification. Each field in the form is an attribute of a class. A typical format of a SMM form is illustrated again in Figure 8.1.

Attributes are split into *public, protected* and *private*. *Public* attributes should be present in all forms filled in during the maintenance task. The software manager should then define the *protected* and *private* attributes which are relevant to the specific software system that is going to be maintained.

Public attributes comprise the basic information about a particular SMM form: the form identification (to enable every single form to be traced throughout the maintenance process), the date of its creation, and the author who created that special form. In addition, as COMFORM also emphasizes the application of the software configuration management discipline, version control during the maintenance process should be applied to all forms filled in. Thus the fields of the *status* section of the SMM forms are part of the public definition as well. The *public* attributes for version control are: status, status date and the person responsible for the status of the form.

As well as *public* attributes, the software manager may wish to export additional attributes of a special class, which can be used ex-

clusively by its subclasses, these attributes are labeled as *protected*.
The objective of having *protected* attributes is to allow generalization
of common attributes to be inherited by subsequent subclasses of a
certain application domain.

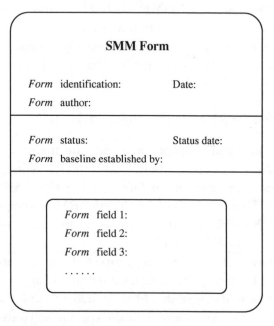

Figure 8.1: Pattern of SMM forms

Private attributes are specific to each SMM form, which are related to certain phases of the methodology (see enclosed square in
Figure 8.1). They are only used in a particular version of a form and
cannot be inherited by the next versions (subclasses) of the form.

Such a strategy given to implement COMFORM increases its lever-
age to support the evolution of a maintenance environment in compliance with the methodology. In this way, the task of documenting
legacy systems can be customized to the maintenance and redocumentation needs of several profiles of software systems. This is accomplished as the software manager is permitted to choose the *protected* and *private* attributes that are relevant to the specific needs to

maintain and document particular software systems.

An example using a `change approval` form which could be generated by the software manager is portrayed in Figure 8.2. In this figure, the definition of a `change approval` form contains the necessary information so that the form serves as one of the documents used as the basis for planning the system release. It should be a vehicle for recording information about software defects, requested enhancements and quality improvements. By documenting new software requirements or those not being met, the `change approval` form may become the contract between the person requesting the change and the maintainers who carry out that change.

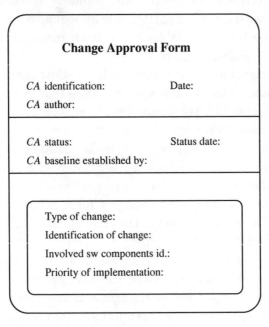

Figure 8.2: `change approval` form

8.1.2. Inheritance Mechanism for Version Control of Forms

Pre-defined forms can be changed either to better support legacy systems being maintained under COMFORM as well as to accommodate other software profiles. Thus, version control of the pre-defined forms has to be considered. The objective in doing this is to create a maintenance knowledge base to serve specific application domains. In order to achieve such flexibility, the concept of inheritance is applied.

The notion of inheritance plays a key role during the version control of pre-defined forms by helping the software manager to derive new versions of forms from primitive ones, by exploiting their commonalities in terms of attributes, and building up class hierarchies. Furthermore, versioning is a particularly appealing technique for managing class evolution as it enables the software manager to try different paths when modelling the forms.

New versions of forms are likely to have additional *protected* and *private* attributes which can be specified from that level to subsequent subclasses. Eventually, the hierarchy of versions becomes somewhat similar to a class hierarchy. *Public* attributes include those which are common to most of the versions, while *private* and *protected* attributes contain variations which are associated with a specific version and a particular application domain respectively.

The software manager may change a form either to add or delete form fields. The reorganization of the class hierarchies involves changing inheritance relationships, adding new *public* or *private* attributes or shifting attributes in the class hierarchies. Supposing that at the time the software manager created the `change approval` form (see Figure 8.2), cost estimation of changes was not taken into account. However, such information has been later found necessary as these estimates are important to project management and can also be used as references for similar work on other projects, or future system releases. Therefore, a new version of the original form is needed.

The creation of a version of a form, using the concept of inheritance, enables the transportation of the *public* attributes regarding identification and version control to the newly versioned form. The *private* attributes of the previous versions could be changed to *protected* and be inherited by the newly generated subclass. On top of that, the attributes related to resource estimation are added to the updated `change approval` form producing a new subclass of the existing one. The resultant form is indicated in Figure 8.3.

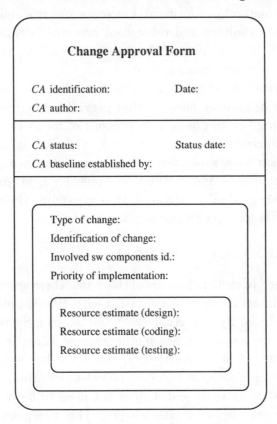

Figure 8.3: Version of a `change approval` form

A lot of work has been done on object-oriented design and implementation. Nevertheless, this section has shown that object-orientation can also be applied to aid the process of maintaining legacy systems. The presented framework encourages the software manager to follow an object-oriented fashion during the definition of form fields at the same time benefiting from features such as inheritance and meta-definition of forms.

It has been felt that the basic reusability issues this strategy encourages would form a useful basis for supporting maintenance and evolution of software systems of several profiles. The framework considers a class hierarchy of forms and incorporates reusability as a natural part of the evolving and refinement process of defining the form fields through the use of the inheritance mechanism, thus applying reusability to software maintenance.

Inheritance allows the creation of new versions of forms which are specialization of existing ones, so that previous experience is reused. The approach given to create new versions of forms is quite natural under object-orientation since a version is viewed as a subclass or a specialization of a superclass. As the maintenance process of a legacy system evolves and matures, the reusable fields of the related set of forms are gradually increased; thus expanding the maintenance knowledge base for a particular application domain.

8.2. On MOOD and COMFORM

As discussed in earlier chapters of this book, there are design trends which try to integrate object-orientation with different methodologies such as Structured System Analysis [46] and Jackson System Development [59]. There are also other methodologies which lead to implementation using Ada. Nevertheless, this book has sought to show that only one approach, in this case object-orientation, is enough to produce software systems and it does not need to be complemented with other approaches or methodologies. This viewpoint encourages software engineers to adhere to the object-oriented paradigm and to benefit from features such as abstraction, encapsulation, inheritance and reusability, from the beginning of software development.

MOOD produces a design by progressive refinement, adding details to the same design model which is strictly object-oriented, and remains consistent through the design phase. Another result of the methodology has been the creation of a graphical notation to represent a design, which makes use of class hierarchy diagrams, composition diagrams, object diagrams and operation diagrams. In addition, since the use of MOOD results in an object-oriented design, it embodies many of the benefits claimed to be inherent in any object-oriented software, such as clarity, modularity and extensibility.

Methodologies are especially important for constructing large scale software. Only recently however, have object-oriented methodologies been exposed to many software engineers. MOOD has been employed to teach object-orientation and design a number of medium size software systems, but naturally the methodology can evolve and mature from further experience with its application to build large software. So far, MOOD has proved to be beneficial and has led to a better understanding of the object-oriented design process.

The MOOD approach to designing could be thought of as being a rigorous one as it lies between an informal and a formal line. Informal methods are based on narrative descriptions but suffer from the ambiguity intrinsic in the use of a natural language. Rigorous approaches have a well-defined syntax and may not be ambiguous. However, they do not have a well-defined semantics so it is difficult to prove their correctness. Formal methods can derive proofs by rules of logic that a design is correct, but they are difficult to be applied by ordinary software engineers. As currently defined and practiced, MOOD is a pragmatic and systematic approach to designing software systems.

There are also many diverse strategies to software maintenance and as such, there is no generally accepted methodology for maintaining legacy systems. In this book, a process model for software maintenance has been described, centered on the software configuration management discipline and incremental redocumentation of existing software, allowing support for a wide range of software maintenance activities. Within this process, reverse engineering supplies the maintainer with a design view of the source code, in order to facilitate reasoning about the code. It is important to note that reverse engineering is not just an optional activity, as in many cases, it provides the only way of discerning the functionality of the source code. In some cases documentation relating to the code is unavailable or simply has not been maintained along with the code. Under such circumstances reverse engineering plays a vital role in enabling effective maintenance.

COMFORM can naturally mature from further experience with its application to maintain sizeable systems over a period of years. The outcome of such experiences will result in a better understanding of the methodology as well as allow its improvement. Up to now, this methodology has led to a better discernment of object-oriented software maintenance.

This book has also shown how object-orientation can permeate the entire software life cycle and affect the engineering of software in one way or another. Hitherto, there is no object-oriented life cycle model that has yet gained general acceptance. However, by trying to incorporate the advantages of an object-oriented approach encompassing MOOD and COMFORM, a coherent life cycle, linking system analysis, domain analysis, design (static and dynamic), implementation and maintenance to form a *seamless* software life cycle model has been presented.

8.3. The Future

With a topic as broad as object-orientation, whose literature offers a myriad of different interpretations and points of view, it has been difficult to give a precise definition for object-oriented concepts. Since there have been many subtle flavours which might be combined to give the overall picture of an object-oriented framework, it has been better to characterize an object-oriented approach. Therefore, this book started by giving a characterization of an object-oriented model based on what the authors felt to be its most relevant concepts (such as classes, objects and inheritance, and their background) along with the philosophy of object-oriented design.

The first chapters of this book faced object-orientation from a methodological standpoint, rather than from an implementation viewpoint. The book was prompted by the perceived inadequacy of existing methodologies to teach object-oriented thinking, and has sought to establish a viable and comprehensive object-oriented design methodology that obtains the benefits of object-orientation, such as encapsulation and inheritance.

There have been many claims about object-thinking regarding power of representation, maintainability, clarity and correctness of object-oriented software. However, at present few of such allegations can be fully validated because most of the attention has been focussed on the implementation phase. From the point of view of programming languages, the road to object-orientation is an evolutionary step, whereas from the point of view of software development methodologies, the differences which exist between traditional structured methods (based on functional decomposition) and those based on object-oriented thinking suggest that a revolution is taking place.

Although a number of object-oriented design methodologies are becoming available and gaining increasing use, so as to answer a broad range of software engineering questions, such methodologies are still at a relatively early stage of growth. Many software engineers still hesitate to use new technologies. An object-oriented transition process [108] encompasses three stages: pre-project planning, technology insertion activities, and project management stage.

It is clear that even more experimentation is required (particularly in developing very large systems) before this paradigm can claim to be a mature subject. Moreover, further experiments will provide several case studies to evaluate the various allegations made about object-thinking, which can only be fully tested when applied to producing substantial software. In fact, considerable experience is being accumulated with the application of object-oriented thinking to developing virtual reality, multimedia and the next generation operating systems.

The outcome of such experiences will progress towards a better understanding of the strengths and weaknesses of object-orientation to create software and might also result in a re-evaluation of some claims made about it in recent years. Therefore, extra experimentations are expected to lead to a better understanding of object-oriented methodologies independent of any programming language, the consolidation of object-oriented concepts and terms, the dissemination of well-accepted notations and the appearance of several libraries of reusable software components for certain application domains.

Despite the existence of considerable amount of information concerning metrics, until now, there are no widely accepted metrics for evaluating object-oriented designs in terms of their complexity, quality, size and schedule. Therefore, new directions in metrics are needed to cater for the features of object-oriented software and reusability. Another issue which could be examined is whether new variations of software metrics can be applied to object-orientation to improve the predictability regarding time and costs involved in object-oriented software development. The number of constructs in an object-oriented design (for instance, the number of operations and attributes for each class) could be used to estimate the size of a system and be good predictors of the total effort necessary to its implementation, and eventually in its maintenance. It has been argued that when object-orientation is used, it is easier to estimate at early stages of the software life cycle the time and costs involved in the whole software development, because of the traceability from design through maintenance.

Software is prone to design faults because, despite modern software development methodologies, most systems continue to be enormously complex. Software engineers should be forced to think about which exceptions might occur and what should be done with them before the implementation phase, and this may lead to the uncovering of more faults during the design phase than might otherwise have been the case.

One reason for applying a fault tolerance strategy is that software creation involves several tasks where there is a significant risk of human and machine faults occurring. Since human beings can make mistakes, software development is therefore susceptible to human faults. Nevertheless, software should be robust enough to deal as far as possible with human and machine faults. A robust software is one which continues to behave reasonably and in a well-defined manner even in the presence of a fault. If a software system is unable to deal with some exceptional conditions, at least it should report the failure and avoid harmful consequences.

If software engineers figure out exceptional conditions during the design phase, it becomes easy to map these exceptions into a programming language during the implementation phase, although the complexity of the design is increased. Therefore, the effect of exception handling in object-oriented software must be taken into account, and the inclusion of exception treatment as part of the design process is tremendously beneficial.

8.4. In Conclusion

As with most topics in computer science, a multitude of additional research fields can easily be identified. The most important topics following from the authors' work have been outlined above. Although the object-oriented paradigm has an evidential learning curve and the adoption of object-orientation does not represent the solution for all software engineering problems, the authors are confident that this paradigm is here to stay because it is a step towards better software quality and reusability.

The idea of software reuse based on the exploitation of the inheritance and composition mechanisms during the design and maintenance phases has been explained in this book. Reusability is a technique for improving software productivity and quality; thus it is finally finding general acceptance. Object-oriented thinking encourages software reuse because it provides special facilities, such as inheritance and encapsulation, making reusability feasible. This suggests that object-orientation may contribute significantly to the solution of the so-called *software crisis*.

The object-oriented paradigm is such a powerful set of concepts that eventually it will get completely absorbed into the software development culture, in the same way that structured methods and to some extent abstract data types concepts have been. This is evident in the abundance of research looking at various aspects of this paradigm. Consequently, the end of the 1990s is likely to be a period of gradual acceptance of object-orientation, which will become the main approach to developing software beyond the turn of this century.

The future of object-oriented software engineering might well be to accept a hybrid trend with other approaches and mapping of concepts between different lines of thought. However, the authors believe that object-oriented thinking should (and hopefully will!) pervade the entire software life cycle. The object-oriented paradigm has required an organized and disciplined view of software development, and has been extended to cover all phases of the software life cycle. This book is believed to teach important steps to understand and promote object-oriented software design and maintenance methodologies.

Exercises

1. Analyze the contradictions (reality and illusion, dreams and nightmares!) of the software engineering discipline.

2. Which objectives should guide a software engineer to design a maintainable object-oriented software?

3. Explain why adopting an object-oriented approach is likely to produce maintainable software.

4. "A design should explicitly deal with all exceptional situations". Is it possible?

5. "Who needs metrics anyway?" Discuss.

6. "Software engineering is just programming". Discuss.

7. "Object-oriented design is easy". Discuss.

8. "Object-oriented thinking is new and revolutionary". Argue.

9. "The object-oriented paradigm is not a panacea". Comment.

10. "Once we have discovered the perfect object-oriented methodology, perfect object-oriented software will be designed every time". Argue.

11. "Reusability will play a key factor to improve software development productivity in the next decade". Comment.

12. "Evidence suggests that there are enormous differences between software engineers in terms of productivity due to psychological aspects and their personality". Comment.

13. "The object-oriented paradigm will be part of the computing mainstream beyond the turn of this century". Comment.

References

1. O.-J. Dahl, B. Myhrhaug, and K. Nygaard. Simula-67 common base language. Technical Report S-22, Norwegian Computing Centre, Oslo, Norway, October 1970.
2. C. A. R. Hoare. Monitors: an operating systems structuring concept. *Communications of the ACM*, 17(10), pp. 549–577, October 1974.
3. B. Liskov, Snyder A., R. Atkinson, and C. Schaffert. Abstraction mechanisms in CLU. *Communications of the ACM*, 20(8), pp. 564–576, August 1977.
4. M. Minsky. A framework for representing knowledge. In P. Wiston, editor, *The Psychology of Computer Vision*. McGraw-Hill, New York, 1975.
5. G. D. Buzzard and T. N. Mudge. Object-based computing and the Ada language. *Computer*, 18(3), pp. 11–19, March 1985.
6. A. Goldberg and D. Robson. *Smalltalk-80: The Language and its Implementation*. Addison-Wesley, Reading, Massachusetts, 1983.
7. D. L. Parnas. On the criteria to be used in decomposing systems into modules. *Communications of the ACM*, 15(12), pp. 1053–1058, December 1972.
8. D. A. Moon. Object-oriented programming with Flavors. In N. Meyrowitz, editor, *Proceedings of the Conference on Object-Oriented Programming: Systems, Languages and Applications - OOPSLA'86*, pp. 1–8, Portland, Oregon, September 1986. ACM SIGPLAN Notices, 21(11), November 1986.
9. M. Stefik and D. G. Bobrow. Object-oriented programming: Themes and variations. *The AI Magazine*, 6(4), pp. 40–62, April 1986.
10. L. G. DeMichiel and R. P. Gabriel. The Common Lisp object system: An overview. In J. Bézivin, J.-M. Hullot, P. Cointe, and H. Liberman, editors, *Proceedings of the European Conference on Object-Oriented Programming - ECOOP'87*, volume 276

of *Lecture Notes in Computer Science*, pp. 151–170, Springer-Verlag, 1987.

11. B. J. Cox. *Object-Oriented Programming - An Evolutionary Approach*. Addison-Wesley, Readings, Massachusetts, 1986.

12. B. Stroustrup. *The C++ Programming Language*. Addison-Wesley, Reading, Massachusetts, 1992.

13. L. Tesler. Object Pascal Report. Technical report, Apple Computer, Santa Clara, California, 1985.

14. L. Cardelli. Modula-3 Report. Technical report, Systems Research Center of Digital Equipment Corporation, Palo Alto, California, 1989.

15. G. Agha. An overview of Actor languages. *ACM SIGPLAN Notices*, 21(10), pp. 58–67, October 1986.

16. P. America. POOL-T: A parallel object-oriented language. In A. Yonezawa and M. Tokoro, editors, *Object-Oriented Concurrent Programming*, pp. 199–220. The MIT Press, Cambridge, Massachusetts, 1987.

17. T. P. Hopkins and M. I. Wolczko. Writing concurrent object-oriented programs using Smalltalk-80. *The Computer Journal*, 32(4), pp. 341–350, August 1989.

18. B. B. Kristensen, O. L. Madsen, B. Moller-Pedersen, and K. Nygaard. Multi-sequential execution in the Beta programming language. *ACM SIGPLAN Notices*, 20(4), pp. 57–70, April 1985.

19. C. Schaffert. An introduction to Trellis/Owl. In N. Meyrowitz, editor, *Proceedings of the Conference on Object-Oriented Programming: Systems, Languages and Applications - OOPSLA'86*, pp. 9–16, Portland, Oregon, September 1986. ACM SIGPLAN Notices, 21(11), November 1986.

20. B. Meyer. *Object-Oriented Software Construction*. Prentice-Hall, Englewood Cliffs, New Jersey, 1988.

21. B. Kirkerud. *Object-Oriented Programming with Simula*. Addison-Wesley, Wokingham, England, 1989.

22. A. Goldberg. *Smalltalk-80: The Interactive Programming Environment*. Addison-Wesley, Reading, Massachusetts, 1984.

23. P. A. Lee and C. Phillips. *The Apprentice C++ Programmer: A Touch of Class*. International Thomson Computer Press, London, 1996.

24. E. H. Khan, M. Al-A'ali, and M. R. Girgis. Object-oriented programming for structured procedural programmers. *Computer*, 28(10), pp. 48–57, 1995.

25. T. Rentsch. Object oriented programming. *ACM SIGPLAN Notices*, 17(9), pp. 51–57, September 1982.

26. D. Thomas. What's in an object. *Byte*, 14(3), pp. 231–240, March 1989.

27. K. Nygaard. Basic concepts in object oriented programming. *ACM SIGPLAN Notices*, 21(10), pp. 128–132, October 1986.

28. P. Wegner. Dimensions of object-based language design. In N. Meyrowitz, editor, *Proceedings of the Conference on Object-Oriented Programming: Systems, Languages and Applications - OOPSLA'87*, pp. 168–182, Orlando, Florida, October 1987. ACM SIGPLAN Notices, 22(12), December 1987.

29. J. O. Guimaraes. The object oriented model and its advantages. *OOPS Messenger*, 6(1), pp. 40–49, January 1995.

30. R. Bellinzona, M. G. Fugini, and B. Percini. Reusing specifications in OO applications. *IEEE Software*, 12(2), pp. 65–75, March 1995.

31. H. Mili, F. Mili, and A. Mili. Reusing software: Issues and research directions. *IEEE Transactions on Software Engineering*, 21(6), pp. 528–562, June 1995.

32. D. Garlan, R. Allen, and J. Ockerbloom. Architectural mismatch: Why reuse is so hard. *IEEE Software*, 12(6), pp. 17–26, November 1995.

33. W. B. Frakes and C. J. Fox. Sixteen questions about software reuse. *Communications of the ACM*, 38(6), pp. 75–87, June 1995.

34. W. Tracz. Software reuse myths. *Software Engineering Notes*, 13(1), pp. 18–22, January 1988.

35. D. Cowan and C. J. P. Lucena. Abstract data views: An interface specification concept to enhance design for reuse. *IEEE Transactions on Software Engineering*, 21(3), pp. 229–243, March 1995.

36. W. C. Lim. Effects of reuse on quality, productivity and economics. *IEEE Software*, 11(5), pp. 23–30, September 1994.

37. W. W. Royce. Managing the development of large software systems. In *Proceedings of the Ninth International Conference on Software Enginnering*, pp. 328–338, Monterey, California, March 1987. IEEE Computer Society Press.

38. B. W. Boehm. A spiral model of software development and enhancement. *Computer*, 21(5), pp. 61–72, May 1988.

39. B. Henderson-Sellers and J. M. Edwards. The object-oriented systems life cycle. *Communications of the ACM*, 33(9), pp. 142–159, September 1990.

40. G. Booch. *Object-Oriented Analysis and Design with Applications*. Benjamin/Cummings, Redwood City, California, 1994.

41. E. Yourdon and L. L. Constantine. *Structured Design*. Prentice-Hall, Englewood Cliffs, New Jersey, 1979.

42. N. Wirth. Program development by stepwise refinement. *Communications of the ACM*, 14(4), pp. 221–227, April 1971.

43. M. A. Jackson. *Principles of Program Design*. Academic Press, New York, New York, 1975.

44. P. P. Chen. The entity-relationship model: Toward a unified view of data. *ACM Transactions on Database Systems*, 1(1), pp. 9–36, March 1976.

45. T. DeMarco. *Structured Analysis and System Specification*. Prentice-Hall, Englewood Cliffs, New Jersey, 1979.

46. C. Gane and T. Sarson. *Structured System Analysis: Tools and Techniques*. Prentice-Hall, Englewood Cliffs, New Jersey, 1979.

47. D. Teichroew and E. A. Hersey. PSL/PSA: A computer-aided technique for structured documentation and analysis of information processing systems. *IEEE Transactions on Software Engineering*, 3(1), pp. 41–48, January 1977.

48. R. J. Lauber. Development support systems. *Computer*, 15(5), pp. 36–46, May 1982.

49. I. Juhani. Object-orientation as structural, functional and behavioural modelling: A comparison of six methods for object-oriented analysis. *Information and Software Technology*, 37(3), pp. 155–163, March 1995.

50. P. Coad and E. Yourdon. *Object-Oriented Analysis*. Prentice-Hall, Englewood Cliffs, New Jersey, 1990.

51. S. Shlaer and S. J. Mellor. *Object Lifecycles: Modeling the World in States*. Prentice-Hall, Englewood Cliffs, New Jersey, 1992.

52. G. Booch. Object-oriented development. *IEEE Transactions on Software Engineering*, 12(2), pp. 211–221, February 1986.

53. E. Seidewitz. General object-oriented software development: Background and experience. *The Journal of Systems and Software*, 9(2), pp. 95–108, February 1989.

54. M. Heitz. HOOD reference manual, issue 3.0. Technical report, European Space Agency, Noordwijk, The Netherlands, September 1989.

55. P. Jalote. Functional refinement and nested objects for object-oriented design. *IEEE Transactions on Software Engineering*, 15(3), pp. 264–270, March 1989.

56. A. I. Wasserman, P. A. Pircher, and R. J. Muller. The object-oriented structured design notation for software design representation. *Computer*, 23(3), pp. 50–63, March 1990.

57. P. Masiero and F. S. R. Germano. JSD as an object-oriented design method. *Software Engineering Notes*, 13(3), pp. 22–23, July 1988.

58. M. E. C. Hull, A. Zarca-Aliabadi, and D. A. Guthrie. Object-oriented design, Jackson System Development (JSD) specification and concurrency. *Software Engineering Journal*, 4(2), pp. 79–86, March 1989.

59. M. A. Jackson. *System Development*. Prentice-Hall, London, 1983.

60. S. C. Bailin. An object-oriented requirements specification method. *Communications of the ACM*, 32(5), pp. 608–623, May 1989.

61. D. M. Bulman. An object-based development model. *Computer Language*, 6(8), pp. 49–59, August 1989.

62. B. Alabiso. Transformation of data flow analysis model to object-oriented design. In N. Meyrowitz, editor, *Proceedings of the Conference on Object-Oriented Programming: Systems, Languages and Applications - OOPSLA'88*, pp. 335–353, San Diego, California, September 1988. ACM SIGPLAN Notices, 23(11), November 1988.

63. P. Ward. How to integrate object orientation with structured analysis and design. *IEEE Software*, 6(2), pp. 74–82, March 1989.

64. R. Wirfs-Brock, B. Wilkerson, and L. Wiener. *Designing Object-Oriented Software*. Prentice Hall, Englewood Cliffs, New Jersey, 1990.

65. J. Rumbaugh, M. Blaha, W. Premerlani, F. Eddy, and W. Lorensen. *Object-Oriented Modeling and Design*. Prentice Hall, Englewood Cliffs, New Jersey, 1991.

66. I. Jacobson. Object oriented development in an industrial environment. In N. Meyrowitz, editor, *Proceedings of the Conference on Object-Oriented Programming: Systems, Languages and Applications - OOPSLA'87*, pp. 183–191, Orlando, Florida, October 1987. ACM SIGPLAN Notices, 22(12), December 1987.

67. R. J. Abbott. Programming design by informal english description. *Communications of the ACM*, 26(11), pp. 882–894, November 1983.

68. G. Booch. *Software Engineering with Ada*. Benjamin/Cummings, Menlo Park, California, 1983.

69. D. W. Embley, B. D. Kurtz, and S. N. Woodfield. *Object-Oriented Systems Analysis: A Model-Driven Approach*. Prentice-Hall, Englewood Cliffs, New Jersey, 1992.

70. W. W. Y Pun and R. L. Winder. A design method for object-oriented programming. In S. Cook, editor, *Proceedings of the European Conference on Object-Oriented Programming - ECOOP'89*, pp. 225–240, Nottingham, United Kingdom, July 1989. Cambridge University Press.

71. W. Cunningham and K. Beck. A diagram for object-oriented programs. In N. Meyrowitz, editor, *Proceedings of the Conference on Object-Oriented Programming: Systems, Languages and Applications - OOPSLA'86*, pp. 361–367, Portland, Oregon, September 1986. ACM SIGPLAN Notices, 21(11), November 1986.

72. M. Ackroyd and D. Daum. Graphical notation for object-oriented design and programming. *Journal of Object-Oriented Programming*, 3(5), pp. 18–28, January 1991.

73. L. F. Capretz and P. A. Lee. Object-oriented design: Guidelines and techniques. *Information and Software Technology Journal*, 35(4), pp. 195–206, April 1993.

74. L. F. Capretz. An integrated CASE for Telecom software production in Europe. In *Proceedings of the Third International Conference on Systems Integration (ICSI'94)*, pp. 1050–1055, São Paulo, Brazil, August 1994. IEEE Computer Society Press.

75. L. F. Capretz and P. A. Lee. Reusability and life cycle issues within an object-oriented design methodology. In R. Ege, M. Singh, and B. Meyer, editors, *TOOLS8 - Technology of Object-Oriented Languages and Systems*, pp. 139–150. Prentice Hall, Englewood Cliffs, New Jersey, 1992.

76. B. Adelson and E. Soloway. The role of domain experience in software design. *IEEE Transactions on Software Engineering*, 11(11), pp. 1351–1360, November 1985.

77. IEEE Std 610.12-1990. *IEEE Standard Glossary of Software Engineering Terminology*. IEEE, 1994.

78. K. H. Bennett. Legacy systems: Coping with success. *IEEE Software*, 12(1), pp. 19–23, 1995.

79. E. J. Chikofsky and J. H. Cross II. Reverse engineering and design recovery: A taxonomy. *IEEE Software*, 7(1), pp. 13–17, 1990.

80. K. Lano and H. Haughton. *Reverse Engineering and Software Maintenance - A Practical Approach*. The McGraw-Hill International Series in Software Engineering, 1994.

81. S. C. Choi and W. Scacchi. SOFTMAN: Environment for forward and reverse case. *Information and Software Technology*, 33(9), pp. 664–674, 1991.

82. S. Burson, G. Kotik, and L. Markosian. A program transformation approach to automating software reengineering. *Reasoning Systems Incorporated, Palo Alto, California, USA*, 1992.

83. K. H. Bennett. Automated support of software maintenance. *Information and Software Technology*, 33(1), pp. 74–85, 1991.

84. C. Desclaux and M. Ribault. MACS: Maintenance assistance capability for software a K.A.D.M.E. In *Proceedings of the Conference on Software Maintenance-1991*, pp. 2–12, Sorrento, Italy, 1991.

85. M. Ward and K. H. Bennett. Formal methods for legacy systems. *Journal of Software Maintenance: Research and Practice*, 7(3), pp. 203–219, 1995.

86. B. P. Lientz and E. F. Swanson. *Software Maintenance Management*. Addison-Wesley, 1980.

87. E. Horowitz and R. C. Williamson. SODOS: A software documentation support environment - its definition. *IEEE Transactions on Software Engineering*, 12(8), pp. 849–859, 1986.

88. P. K. Garg and W. Scacchi. A hypertext system to manage software life-cycle documents. *IEEE Software*, 7(3), pp. 90–98, 1990.

89. K. Wong, S. R. Tilley, H. A. Müller, and M. D. Storey. Structural redocumentation: A case study. *IEEE Software*, 12(1), pp. 46–54, 1995.

90. W. A. Babich. *Software Configuration Management - Coordination for Team Productivity*. Addison-Wesley, 1986.

91. E. H. Bersoff, V. D. Henderson, and S. G. Siegel. *Software Configuration Management - An Investment in Product Integrity.* Prentice-Hall, 1980.

92. M. J. Rochkind. The source code control system. *IEEE Transactions on Software Engineering*, 1(4), pp. 364–370, 1975.

93. W. F. Tichy. RCS - a system for version control. *Software - Practice and Experience*, 15(7), pp. 637–654, July 1985.

94. S. I. Feldman. Make - a program for maintaining computer programs. *Software Practice and Experience*, 9, pp. 255–265, 1979.

95. B. W. Boehm. Software engineering. *IEEE Transactions on Computer*, 25(12), pp. 1226–1241, 1976.

96. C. Liu. A look at software maintenance. *Datamation*, 22(11), pp. 51–55, 1976.

97. S. S. Yau and J. S. Collofello. Some stability measures for software maintenance. *IEEE Transactions on Software Engineering*, 6(6), pp. 545–552, 1980.

98. J. Martin and C. McClure. *Software Maintenance - The Problem and Its Solutions.* Prentice Hall, 1983.

99. B. H. Patkau. A foundation for software maintenance. MSc thesis, University of Toronto, Toronto, Canada, December 1983.

100. L. J. Arthur. *Software Evolution - The Software Maintenance Challenge.* John Wiley & Sons, 1988.

101. J. R. Foster, A. E. P. Jolly, and M. T. Norris. An overview of software maintenance. *British Telecom Technology Journal*, 7(4), pp. 37–46, 1989.

102. S. L. Pfleeger and S. A. Bohner. A framework for software maintenance metrics. In *Proceedings of the Conference on Software Maintenance-1990*, pp. 320–327, San Diego, California, 1990.

103. K. H. Bennett, B. Cornelius, M. Munro, and D. Robson. Software maintenance. In J. A. McDermid, editor, *Software Engineer's Reference Book.* Butterworth-Heinemann, 1991.

104. D. S. Hinley and K. H. Bennett. Using a model to manage the software maintenance process. In *Proceedings of the Conference*

on *Software Maintenance-1992*, pp. 174–182, Florida, 1992.

105. M. A. M. Capretz and M. Munro. Software configuration management issues in the maintenance of existing systems. *Journal of Software Maintenance: Research and Practice*, 6(1), pp. 1–14, 1994.

106. G. Canfora, A. Cimitile, and M. Munro. RE2: Reverse-engineering and reuse re-engineering. *Journal of Software Maintenance: Research and Practice*, 6(2), pp. 53–72, March 1994.

107. M. A. M. Capretz and L. F. Capretz. The object-oriented paradigm for software evolution. In *Proceedings of the 18th Annual International Computer Software and Applications Conference (COMPSAC'94)*, pp. 23–28, Taipei, Taiwan, 1994. IEEE Computer Society Press.

108. M. E. Fayad, W. T. Tsai, and M. Fulghum. Transition to object-oriented software development. *Communications of the ACM*, 39(2), pp. 108–121, February 1996.

Index